11.6.'21

Happy Birthday

Love from Colives.

C000186973

A CLEAR CASE OF GENIUS

The phrase 'a clear case of genius' is taken from a letter of 17 March 1918 from the American Ambassador in London, Dr Walter Hines Page, to President Woodrow Wilson.

A CLEAR CASE OF GENIUS

ROOM 40's CODE-BREAKING PIONEER

ADMIRAL SIR REGINALD 'BLINKER' HALL

WITH COMMENTARY BY PHILIP VICKERS

The History Press

To my parents, Frances Alice and Reginald Henry Vickers, who survived two world wars and introduced me to Jules Verne's *The Mysterious Document*, *The Cryptogram* and *Mathias Sandorf*, which first generated my interest in secret intelligence.

O voyagers, O seamen,
You who came to port, and you whose bodies
Will suffer the trial and judgement of the sea,
Or whatever event, this is your real destination […]
Not fare well,
But fare forward, voyagers.

T.S. Eliot, 'The Dry Salvages', *Four Quartets*

Frontispiece: Admiral Sir Reginald Hall. (Sketch by Louis Raemaker/T. Stubbs, CAC)

First published 2017

The History Press
The Mill, Brimscombe Port
Stroud, Gloucestershire, GL5 2QG
www.thehistorypress.co.uk

Autobiography © Reginald Hall, 2017
Commentary and supporting text © Philip Vickers, 2017

The right of Reginald Hall and Philip Vickers to be identified as the Authors of this work has been asserted in accordance with the Copyright, Designs and Patents Act 1988.

British Library Cataloguing in Publication Data.
A catalogue record for this book is available from the British Library.

ISBN 978 0 7509 8265 8

Typesetting and origination by The History Press
Printed and bound in Great Britain by TJ International Ltd

CONTENTS

FOREWORD

In a past intelligence world apparently populated almost exclusively by colourful and engaging characters, 'Blinker' Hall cut a remarkable figure as an innovator, administrator and politician. He is rightly credited with having supervised some of the most successful clandestine operations of the First World War and, most importantly, of creating and nurturing Britain's first dedicated cryptographic organisation. His name is immediately associated with the code-breakers of Room 40, the development of the cryptanalytical techniques which cracked the German Foreign Ministry's diplomatic cypher, and with the foundation of a highly specialised branch of covert warfare.

Much has been written about Hall, in part because of what his division of the Admiralty accomplished on his watch, but when in his retirement he entered politics few outsiders knew very much at all about what his very 'unnaval' collection of eccentric academics, playwrights, actors and novelists had achieved equipped with just paper and pencil. The full background of, for example, the decryption of the Zimmermann Telegram, or the interception of the *Kaisermarine*'s cypher system, would not be disclosed for years in the anticipation that such measures could be required in a future conflict. Understandably, successive British governments sought to impose discretion on the cognoscenti, but that effort was doomed when litigation initiated in the United States, far outside Whitehall's jurisdictional reach, threatened to reveal the scale of Britain's investment in eavesdropping.

So many years later, following revelations about the impact of Bletchley Park on the Allies' successful prosecution of the Second World War, and even more recent indiscretions about the role of its successor organisation, Government Communications Headquarters, Hall's role acquires a special status among the pantheon of British Intelligence. Now, at last, we can get an insight into what he thought about some of the historic events to which he was witness.

Nigel West
2017

INTRODUCTION

One distinctive figure stands centre stage in any line-up of Intelligence Chiefs, a man with eyes that blinked rapidly. He was Admiral Sir Reginald 'Blinker' Hall, Director of Naval Intelligence (DNI) throughout the First World War and chief of Room 40, his headquarters in the Admiralty.

Room 40 has been credited by many as being the most successful intelligence operation of all time, and as Winston Churchill observed of Hall's worldwide network in *The World Crisis*, 'There were others – a brilliant confederacy – whose names even now are better wrapt in mystery'. This comment was true when written in 1923, and remains so today. Several biographies of Hall, and many histories of British secret intelligence agencies, have brought his name before the general public, yet he remains an enigmatic figure. This should not surprise us on two counts.

First, it is in the nature of secret services that much more remains hidden than is available to the wider public. Second, Hall's autobiography was banned by order of the government and was mostly destroyed. Only seven draft chapters out of the thirty he contemplated and partly completed survive; and they represent a proportion of the opus he began work on in 1926, but was forced to abandon when the Admiralty intervened in August 1933 and ensured the destruction of Chapters 4, 8–17 and 19–24. Chapter 18 is virtually a duplicate of Chapter 7, and of the missing material we know only that two of them, one of which was Chapter 20, were concerned with Naval Intelligence Division (NID) activities in the western Mediterranean.

Numerous writers have quoted from his extant chapters but it is only now, some eighty years later, that they can be published in full, with some editorial support. What emerges is a fascinating, candid account of clandestine operations that throws some light on why the autobiography came to be banned, ostensibly on security grounds. The surviving manuscript offers a unique insight into the man himself and of the work of Room 40. It highlights strengths and weaknesses and demonstrates that although times may change, the fundamental principles of intelligence collection remain relevant to today's challenges.

Hall presents a particular picture of the First World War era, and tells us much about the ninety-three extraordinary and colourful characters who inhabited, and were involved with, his organisation which routinely handled issues of maritime trade, economics, contraband and, of course, cryptography and covert operations. Many of his subordinates who are today quite unknown or forgotten were, at the time, crucial performers in the secret war. These and other individuals have been researched by the editor so as to begin to answer such important questions as: who is Colyn; what part does 'the mysterious Graves' play; what role did the *Deutschland* play; and why is Colonel Cockerill so important?

Hall wrote his autobiography in collaboration with Ralph Straus, the erudite author, particularly noted for his remarkable book *The Unspeakable Curll*. Hall was in very good hands here and, once the ban was imposed, Straus suggested to Hall that the book should be rewritten in the form of a novel. Hall rejected this idea but, had it gone ahead, we would know a great deal more. According to Hall's grandson, Timothy

Stubbs, when Straus died 'a great number of the Admiral's papers were destroyed'. There is also evidence that Hall himself destroyed much of Room 40's papers at the time of its closure in 1919.

For one of his chapters Hall consulted Thoroton on BNI activities in the western Mediterranean. In this correspondence Thoroton refers to a smuggling operation by his agent, Juan March, concerning rifles and ammunition, which were secreted in fake Corinthian columns by March, thus obviating risk of investigation by customs' agents.[1]

Emphatically, this is not another biography of Admiral Hall, nor is it intended to be a further history of Room 40, but it is in part an explanation of why the government sought to suppress the memoirs of a loyal and efficient intelligence professional. At the time, the authorities gave five 'security reasons' why the pages that follow should not be released: concern was expressed about the accurate identification of Hall's staff and colleagues, and there was a fear that his memoirs would compromise sources and methods. His details of the funding of officers working in foreign countries were potentially indiscreet, and there was a broader anxiety about the political climate of the day – when Adolf Hitler was gaining recognition as a threat to Britain's future security. Additionally, there is also an internal Room 40 factor to be considered, that of William Russell Clarke, described by Paul Gannon as a 'barrister, intelligence officer, guardian of the secret', who had been a Room 40 code-breaker since 1916. In 1933 he held the post of Chief Censor at the Admiralty, and he pointed out that certain chapters, relating to the performance of some naval commanders, would only lead to 'the row that is certain to be generated'. As Gannon explained in his *Inside Room 40 – The Code Breakers of World War I*, simple jealousy may have

---

1   Thoroton to Hall correspondence, 1926, TFA.

been a motive, as Clarke, who was 'extremely arrogant and brimming with sarcasm', was planning to write his own account.

The ban not only affected Hall's original manuscript, but seems to have extended to a collection of photographs assembled by Colonel Charles Julian Thoroton, a Royal Marines Light Infantry officer who acted as Hall's Chief of Intelligence in Gibraltar. Thoroton wrote to Hall about their disappearance on 21 November 1932, but without success.

At least two of Hall's original chapters were devoted to the Iberian Peninsula and Morocco, areas which had come under the ambit of the NID's Gibraltar Station. Hall's collaborator, Ralph Straus, referred these to as 'the Thoroton chapters', and their loss is a tragedy; matters pertaining to Spain and the Mediterranean were of crucial importance to Room 40. The theatre was of great strategic importance, and must have involved trade issues, which dominate many of the NID reports about neutral countries. The smuggling of contraband and the collection of information to support the imposition of embargoes and the compilation of the dreaded Black Lists were all part of the NID's wide area of responsibility. Critical materiel included the components for the manufacture of steel and munitions, the transport of foodstuffs, leatherwork and weapons, as well as horses and mules destined for the combat zones in Europe and the Middle East.

Of great strategic significance in the region were the mines of Rio Tinto, which had been exploited originally in 3000 BC. They were acquired by Hugh Matheson in 1873 in a consortium involving Deutsche Bank and a leading railway company. By the outbreak of war they were under the control of the Rothschilds who expanded them to develop the deposits of bauxite for aluminium, iron ore, copper, uranium, coal and diamonds, which were so significant to the war economy. In the struggle for control of these mines the British triumphed over the Germans and in 1915 Hall's men drew in personnel from the Spanish security agencies to protect the sites from sabotage. One of Hall's Spanish agents, Juan March, held a major financial holding in the Rio Tinto

Company, having been recruited by the Gibraltar Station in competition against their German adversaries. This aspect has been touched on by Patrick Beesly in *Room 40* where he gives an account of the *Erri Berro*, a Brigantine involved in Wolfram-running and the smuggling of anthrax germs.[2] The first fully detailed account of March's collaboration with BNI can be read in *Finding Thoroton*.

Underlying the importance of the autobiography is the opinion of Admiral Sir William James, who served with Hall in HMS *Queen Mary*, and whom Hall appointed his deputy in charge of Room 40 in 1917. James recalled, 'It is evident from the chapter headings of the thirty unwritten chapters that his autobiography would have been a book of historical importance.' Indeed, in the basement of his home at 53 Cadogan Gardens he held 10,000 diplomatic decrypts, which were destroyed. During the war, Hall also lived at 36 Curzon Street in his family apartment.

As for Hall himself, he was born on 28 June 1870 in Salisbury, Wiltshire. His father was Captain William Henry Hall, the first DNI who built up the department from a standing start. His mother Caroline was the daughter of the Reverend Henry Armfield, the Canon of Salisbury Cathedral. Charles Dickens had died only eleven days before Hall's birth, and England, in 1870, was in the throes of major educational developments and radical employment reforms.

On the world scene, 1870 saw the Franco-Prussian War break out with Germany achieving unification under Bismarck. The industrial revolution had made Britain 'the workshop of the world'. The Royal Navy, which Hall was to join in 1883, only one year after the foundation of the Naval Intelligence Division under Admiral Sir George Tryon, was Great Britain's most prized possession.[3]

---

2   This seems to be the only 'missing' chapter to have escaped destruction but *Room 40* by Beesly provides no provenance.

3   See Map 1.

Hall was catapulted from command of the North Sea battlecruiser *Queen Mary*, after the Battle of Heligoland Bight in August 1914, to become Director of Naval Intelligence. His last Sea Chief, Admiral David Beatty, saw this appointment as a 'far more important office' than the one Hall had held under him. The promotion was certainly fortuitous for Hall, as the *Queen Mary* was sunk at the Battle of Jutland on 31 May 1916 with the loss of 1,266 officers and men.

According to those who knew him, Hall possessed a steely authority combined with solicitous concern for his crew; inflexible standards of achievement, softened by a wealth of human empathy; and the ability to weld a heterogeneous group of brilliantly minded and independent men, and women, into a single working caucus.

For example, in the eastern Mediterranean, Blinker appointed Gertrude Margaret Lothian Bell, who was described as the most intelligent woman in Britain. Hall recruited her in 1915 to work in his Cairo Bureau as 'Major Miss Bell', a General Staff officer. The Cairo Bureau was the intelligence centre for Gallipoli. She found old friends there including T.E. Lawrence and Leonard Woolley, who was Intelligence Chief at Port Said, and Hall's own brother, who was in charge of the railway. It was Bell who briefed Winston Churchill in his Middle East politics at the Cairo Conference and it was she who groomed Lawrence in his role as Lawrence of Arabia.

The American Ambassador, Dr Walter Page, in writing to President Woodrow Wilson, remarked:

Hall is one genius the war has developed. Neither in fiction nor in fact can you find any man to match him. Of the wonderful things I know he has done, there are several that it would take an exciting volume to tell. The man is a genius – a clear case of genius. All other secret service men are amateurs by profession. For Hall can look through you and see the very muscular movements of your immortal soul while he is talking to you.[4]

And Page wrote much more in the same vein.

As will become clear, Admiral Hall was a lateral thinker well ahead of his time, and therein lies a clue to his success. He was also deeply committed to truth: truth in passing on Room 40's decrypts so that no ambiguity could arise as to their reliability and at a time when it could do the most good and at the least risk to security. There was no 'sexing-up' in those days and 'spin' was restricted to offensive propaganda to confuse the enemy and not one's own nation. This attitude is made explicit in Chapter 6, 'A Little "Information" for the Enemy'. His lasting reputation, of course, centres on his work in Room 40, credited with bringing the United States into a war that cost 1,150,000 French military deaths, 735,287 British and 116,708 American, but that nonetheless ensured an Allied victory.

Hall himself was a true eccentric, even in his home life, kicking over his wife's tea table after a frustrating day, an incident passed over lightly by her in explaining this event to her somewhat astonished lady friends. His grandson, Timothy Stubbs, recounted an intimate family example: his grandfather's favourite breakfast was 'cold rice pudding followed by cold roast partridge!'

But it is his remarkable reforms on board the navy's warships where his originality showed: the three-watch system; and his introduction of the first chapel, the first library, the first cinema – all innovations to the horror and alarm of diehard naval officers, but later taken up by the fleet altogether. On top of this were his important naval gunnery developments.

Much of the man's character is perceptible in his writing. He is clearheaded, accurate and open. He has a sense of humour. He treats all men equally. There is no sign of bluster, vindictiveness or vainglory. His

---

4   Burton J. Hindrick, *The Life and Letters of Walter H. Page* (USA, 1923).

penetrating gaze and highly developed perception is commented on by everyone who knew him. He held great respect for all who worked with and for him, and even for some who were against him. His admiration for Miss Jane Adams, the American pioneer of women's suffrage, is self-evident. He could even make friends of enemies, as in the case of Franz von Rintelen.

Fortunately, we can gather more personal details of the Admiral through the reminiscence of his grandson, Timothy Stubbs, a naval officer himself. In a letter to the editor, on 11 March 2016, he writes:

Small of stature, with piercing eyes, a staccato way of speaking and a barking laugh; with a profile not unlike Mr Punch. It was thought that the Admiral could hold a piece of toast between the end of his nose and his chin. He sported fabulous dragons, tattooed on either forearm. These are the memories I have of my grandfather, when, as a very small boy, I lived at Dockhead, his house in Beaulieu.

I can recall walking with him in the garden of Dockhead when he always wore a flat cap and a waistcoat from which his monocle used to dangle on a black silk ribbon. He had two particular passions in the garden, a cactus, Dahlia 'Baby Royal' of which there were legion and Alpine strawberries which grew profusely on the sides of a small rill that ran down to the Beaulieu view.

As the Admiral was in poor health when I lived at Dockhead, he spent a deal of time, wreathed in smoke from innumerable Turkish cigarettes, closeted in his study, clacking away on an ancient typewriter, firing off letters to a broad spectrum of friends and ex-colleagues. He also wrote at least once a week to his sister, Mary Templar, to whom he was devoted.

Clearly I had no notion of the 'Admiral's importance in the field of espionage and only remember him as a mainly benevolent, though somewhat alarming Grandfather. If you behaved yourself and did your best, he was always on your side; if you did not life could be painful.

Earlier, Timothy Stubbs had written other personal memoirs, on 21 April 2014:

> The only memorabilia of the Admiral that I have are a pair of ancient ivory-backed hairbrushes and a pair of gold cufflinks decorated with blue enamel anchors. He always wore them. My personal memories are that, for a small boy, he was somewhat alarming, with his piercing blue eyes and a slightly parade ground voice. He was, after all, trained as a gunnery officer. He was very strict and a devil for punctuality; should I (at the age of 7) arrive late for lunch, I would be banished to my bedroom for the rest of the day. He much preferred little girls. My mother was his favourite. Both his sons addressed him as 'Sir' until the day he died. I know that this paints an unfair picture, as he was, I know, a compassionate man who was always greatly concerned with the welfare of those that he commanded. He did, however, demand very high standards.

The Admiral had his portrait painted by Sir Gerald Kelly, PRA ('not very good, I thought,' writes his grandson). Timothy considers a Louis Raemaker sketch to be his best portrait, an opinion I fully concur with as, more than any photograph, the artist brings the man's character alive before our very eyes.

Read in its entirety, Hall's original manuscript gives a better understanding both of the man and of the NID's worldwide network. One question that seems to have been left unanswered by historians is the number of lives saved by Room 40. There are no commonly agreed statistics to support any particular assessment, but there can be little doubt of the overall impact of naval intelligence on the successful prosecution of the war.

The NID worked closely with its military intelligence counterparts at the War Office, and this liaison led Hall to attribute many of his successes to this mutually beneficial relationship. Take, for example, the British secret agent who is alleged to have attended a Berlin reception during the war, and then submitted a report in which he described the German plan for a forthcoming attack on Verdun, code-named Operation GERICHT. Was this the handiwork of the NID or the Directorate of Military Intelligence?

Louise de Bettignies, 'Alice Dubois' of the network code-named RAMBLE and based in the Lille area, had been recruited by Major Walter Kirke in Folkestone to head an eighty-strong organisation behind enemy lines. One of her final messages, before being arrested by the Germans in Froyennes near Tournai in October 1915, disclosed the German plan. The report was forwarded to the French commander at Verdun who refused to believe it, but nevertheless her network is credited with having saved more than 1,000 British lives.

There are other examples where good intelligence was exploited to great advantage. In *Haig's Intelligence: GHQ and the German Army, 1916–1918*, Jim Beach attributes intelligence failures during the Battle of the Somme as in some part contributing to the continued slaughter. On the first day of that battle, thirteen divisions of the British 4th Army suffered some 57,470 casualties, the greatest number ever recorded in British military history. This was followed by Passchendaele with over 300,000 British dead or wounded. It may be argued that the collapse of the RAMBLE network was in some measure a cause of the intelligence vacuum that led to such losses.

Elsewhere on the Western Front the painter Paul Maze, a friend of Winston Churchill, was employed at GHQ, from the age of 21, on the retreat from Mons and all through the war – including Flanders, Ypres, Loos, Passchendaele and Cambrai – to portray the German front line and trench dispositions, made with 'the artist's power of selective visualisation'. He was not a spy as such (but very nearly shot as a German spy by the British!) but a unique observer. He wrote of the first day on the Somme that:

So many fell within minutes or seconds of their leaving their trenches. I was spared that experience but on the evening I was sent to make a report of what I could discover, as news from units engaged had hardly reached the headquarters which had ordered the offensive. Alas the battle never died down until the next spring and there can be few yards of that country where so many fallen men of all ages gave their lives fighting for their country. So many young men straight from England were thrown into battle without having the slightest conception of what they would be facing. Men's lives were short lived indeed.[5]

It may be asked why there is an absence of official information relating to the trade and economic situation prevailing throughout the conflict, and it would seem likely that these topics were also part of Hall's banned autobiography. Trade, economics and financial interests have long been identified as the driving force behind empire building. Empires require armies, as Niall Ferguson observed in *Empire: How Britain Made the Modern World*. At that time the British Empire was at its apogee, governing roughly a quarter of the world's population and the same proportion of the earth's land surface, as well as nearly all its oceans and seas. The British Empire was the greatest empire ever known, protected by the Royal Navy, a force that literally ruled the waves: 40 miles of British warships were reviewed by King George V at Spithead in 1914.

The Merchant Navy carried more than half of the world's seaborne trade, and the freedom of the sea routes was an obvious priority for the Admiralty and His Majesty's government.

In 1914 Americans had been almost totally unaware that war was imminent in Europe. Tens of thousands of American tourists were caught by surprise. Neutrality was the watchword, particularly amongst

---

5   Letter to the editor, 31 January 1975.

Americans of Irish, German and Swedish origin, along with certain church leaders and women. Many of the influential, including the automobile manufacturer Henry Ford, were pacifists. News of German atrocities in Belgium and the sinking of the *Lusitania* in 1915 resulted in a shift of public opinion, which began to see Germany in a rather different light. President Wilson then initiated large-scale loans to Britain and France, and US exports to the belligerent nations rose from $824.8 million in 1913 to $2.5 billion in 1917. Industrial production increased 30 per cent and the US Gross National Product went up by some 20 per cent.

In joining the Allies in April 1917 the Americans not only ensured victory but also saved themselves from the German and Mexican scheme to invade the southern states, thereby preventing great loss of life. Rightly described as the man who brought America into the Great War, the autobiography of 'Blinker' Hall remains a unique testimony to the thinking and methodology of one whom Winston Churchill described as being responsible for 'the most successful intelligence operation of all time'.

HALL'S CHRONOLOGY

NAVAL CAREER

1870 Born in Salisbury, 28 June

1883 Entered Royal Navy, HMS *Britannia*, River Dart

1885 At sea, HMS *Northampton*, North America & West Indian Squadron

1889 Promoted to sub-lieutenant

1890 Lieutenant, HMS *Imperieuse*, China Station

Junior staff, HMS *Excellent*, Whale Island

1894 Married, age 24, Ethel de Wiveslie Abbey

1898 Senior staff officer, HMS *Australia*

1901 Promoted to commander, HMS *Magnificent* and HMS *Cornwallis*

1905 Promoted to captain

1907 Captain, HMS *Cornwall*

1908 First intelligence mission, Kiel Harbour

Captain, HMS *Natal*

1913 Command of HMS *Queen Mary*

WARTIME CAREER

1914 Commands the *Queen Mary* in Heligoland battle

Appointed Director of Naval Intelligence

Initiates postal censorship

Magdeburg cypher key passed by Russians to Room 40

Sayonara sails to Ireland

Vergemere sails to Spain

1915 Battle of the Dogger Bank

Hall initiates a plot to separate Turkey from Germany

Wassmuss's codebooks captured. Room 40 decoding and reading major German codes (codes 1847, 2310 and 89734)

13040 decyphered

Sinking of the *Lusitania*

1916 Battle of Jutland

Takes overall charge of Room 40

Attends Dardanelles Commission

1917 Zimmermann Telegram. The US enters First World War

1918 Sortie of the *Hochseeflotte* (HSF). Mutiny of the HSF

POLITICS AND RETIREMENT

1919 Elected to House of Commons as MP for Liverpool West Derby

1924 Zinoviev Letter

1925 Elected to House of Commons for Eastbourne

1926 Starts work on his autobiography

1929 Retires from Parliament
Moves to the New Forest
Lectures in the USA
1932 His wife, Essie, dies
1933 The Admiralty bans his autobiography
1939 Active in intelligence for Second World War
Joins the Home Guard
1943 In ill health. Dies, age 73, 22 October, in London

1325789
0643741
3690677
4336797
6120995
3258096
3146615
3406232
3680863
1009753

HALL'S ORIGINAL
AUTOBIOGRAPHY

2170097
5346789
9753245
6789086
4544689
8642293
8578132
5789064
3741369
0677433
6797612
0995325
8096314
6615340
6232368
0863100
3678643
3456789
7399753
2456789
0864544
6898642
2938578

THE NATURE OF INTELLIGENCE
WORK

Almost every week sees the publication in this country of some new novel or volume of reminiscences which purports to deal with the activities of the 'Secret Services'. Ingenious novelists build up exciting romances, and if some of their stories are almost ludicrously unlike the real thing, who will blame them? Not I. They are giving the public the kind of entertainment for which it may legitimately ask. Moreover, they do sometimes give you a very fair idea of some part of the truth. Somerset Maugham did it in his *Ashenden*. Temple Thurston did it in his *Portrait of a Spy*. He came to us for some of his facts. In more than one of his novels, too, A. E. W. Mason was writing of intelligence work from knowledge gained at first hand. And if in the works of less responsible writers mysterious blond ladies too often lure impressionable officers to their doom in the least probable manner, it cannot be denied that women are sometimes employed to obtain information, and officers, not only those of junior rank, have been known to be singularly indiscreet. In the memoirs you naturally find a greater measure of sober fact, but even here it is the half-truth that most often provides the 'astounding revelations' so dear to the public. So far, indeed, as intelligence work is concerned I doubt whether one man in ten thousand is ever in a position to be able to tell more than a little piece of the truth. A square, even a dozen squares of the intelligence chessboard, may be as familiar to him as his own reflection in a mirror, but it would require a miracle to enable him to envisage with any accuracy all the sixty-four squares. Nobody, in fact, certainly not myself, is capable of giving anything like a complete picture, however restricted his chosen canvas may be, which is not largely the product of his imagination.

Nevertheless these books continue to be written, and the subject seems to exercise a perennial interest over writers and readers alike. This is hardly surprising. At all times, but particularly during war, those affairs which it is 'not in the public interest' to divulge are more often than not of a highly dramatic nature. They may not embrace a major sensation, but at least they are in the sharpest contrast to the ordinary affairs of everyday life. And the agent or spy who may be concerned in them is not unnaturally invested with that glamour which will always surround those whose work, in the view of the man in the street, bears no resemblance to any work he knows by experience.

Now few enough spies will intrude into these pages of mine. Too many books have already been filled with highly coloured accounts of their activities. Here you will find little more than the tale of a single department. Yet we in the ID [Intelligence Department] had our fill of excitements during those four years of war, even though so much of our time was spent in dull tabulation and dreary waiting. There were coincidences which most writers of fiction would regard as wholly unpardonable. There were crashes of surprise as unexpected as any to be found in the last chapter of a detective story, and sometimes, I freely admit, incidents came to our knowledge which in their sheer fantastic improbability differed not at all from those which you find in the most sensational novels.

Where, for instance, are you likely to meet with a crazier affair than the destruction of the German submarine *U.28*? The official histories have little of any interest to say of *U.28*: she was merely sunk in an explosion on 2 September 1917. But we had the whole story, which, like so many stories of the kind, could not be told at the time and in later days seemed to be forgotten. In point of actual fact *U.28* was sunk by a motor-lorry!

It sounds absurd, a Munchausen yarn, yet it happened. At the time we were sending out considerable quantities of stores and ammunition to Murmansk. One of the ships engaged on this particular job was the SS *Olive Branch*, and on her last voyage she carried on her upper deck a small fleet of motor-lorries. She was stopped by *U.28* off the coast of Norway, and her men were ordered to abandon ship. When they had got safely away the submarine closed on her and put a shell into her after-hold. Unfortunately for them the Germans were ignorant of the fact huge quantities of high explosive had been carefully packed into that hold. The result of the shell-burst was appalling. There came a sudden volcano in angry eruption, the air was full of motor-lorries describing unusual paraboles. And one, the largest of them all, choosing to come down with almost mathematical precision on to the foredeck of the submarine, burst in and drowned her.

This of course is not my story, but it invariably recalls itself to my mind when I am asked whether any of those very tall yarns of the navy, which used to be whispered about, were true. It certainly was the fact that the strangest things were frequently happening, and not only on the high seas: yet I am sometimes inclined to think that perhaps the strangest thing of all was the Intelligence Division itself. For it was like nothing else that had ever existed. It grew, Heaven alone knows just how, from a comparatively minor and purely naval department into an almost worldwide organisation with a multitude of the most diverse activities.[1] And as these activities increased, so did its staff. It was the most wonderful that any man could have hoped to gather about him, but it must have been the most heterogeneous staff that ever came together. Men and

---

1   See map 1.

women of every profession and class joined us, and in many cases they had little but their own good sense to guide them aright. We had few enough precedents to follow, and we had to make our own rules as we went along. We had our successes, but we also had our ignominious failures. And I hope I shall not be misunderstood if I add that we had our comic-opera moments, when it was difficult to realise that we were in the midst of war. But in this respect, I presume, we were not unique.

It is not very easy to know where to begin, but it may be well if I preface these memories of mine with a brief description of the principles underlying the organisation of Intelligence work. There can be no hard and fast rules in the business, but in wartime at any rate there are four cardinal points to be borne in mind. First and foremost there is the acquisition of information about the enemy, and so far as knowing where to look for it is concerned, that is a comparatively simple matter. Then there is the double process of sifting what seems to be the truth from what is probably or demonstrably false, and of knitting together the pieces of information obtained so as to produce a balanced picture: and that is not easy. In the third place, those in authority have to decide how to use the information given them to the best possible advantage, and that is always a troublesome task. Finally there is the necessity for covering up all tracks so that the enemy may remain in ignorance of the fact that any of his secrets have been discovered, and that can be very difficult indeed.

As regards the first point it is a well-known fact now that no nation was so well served by its agents as we were. Before the war some very wonderful results were obtained by men who seldom enough could be adequately rewarded for their long years of patient and unobtrusive and sometimes most dangerous work.[2] Many of their exploits have already

2   See maps 2 and 3.

been related in print: some will never be told. But it did occasionally happen that an amateur was called on to take a hand in the game, and I may perhaps be forgiven if I mention here a personal experience of my own, for it may have had some bearing on my appointment in October 1914 as Director of the Intelligence Division of the Admiralty Staff, a post, by the way, of which my father had been the first holder on its creation in 1882.

Sometime in 1909 while in command of the *Cornwall* I was directed to take a number of cadets for a six month's cruise in the Baltic.[3] I looked forward to a pleasantly light task, but I was soon undeceived. Vice Admiral Sir Francis Bridgeman sent for me to give me detailed instructions, and I then learnt that I would be expected to do very much more than superintend the sea-studies of fifty or sixty cadets. Information was required by the Admiralty on a number of points connected with harbour fortifications and the like, and to provide it would be part of my duties. The cruise, indeed, was an intelligence move. 'And if it turns out to be the success that we hope,' said the Admiral, 'it will not be the worse for W.R. Hall.' I left him determined to wing back the information that was required but without any clear idea as to how it was to be obtained.

Now one of the points about which the Admiralty required accurate information was the length of the building slips at the head of Kiel harbour and what was being built there. Various reports had been made to them, but none had been satisfactory. The Germans were taking unusual precautions to guard this naval secret, and so far these had proved effective.

Well, we had arrived at Kiel early one morning in June, a carefully chosen day for it was Regatta week and the German High Seas fleet

---

3   See map 4.

was ranged in order for it. There had been the usual ceremonial visits, Prince Henry of Prussia, I remember, came aboard and inspected our cadets and everyone was most cordial and friendly. And, to be candid, I felt some reluctance to attempt any intelligence work while accepting their hospitality. But it so happened that I was insulted on my own quarterdeck by no less a person than Grand Admiral von Tirpitz himself, and that was enough to remove any scruples of mine.

There had been a luncheon party on board the *Cornwall* that day, and it was to be followed by an afternoon dance. Prince and Princess Henry and Fraulein von Tirpitz were among our guests. The dance had begun when we were told that the Grand Admiral was coming. He was received with the guard and band, and I stood at the head of the gangway to welcome him, with Fraulein von Tirpitz standing by me. As he came over the side his daughter stepped forward and spoke to him in English. 'Oh, Papa, how nice of you to come!'

He replied in French: '*C'est seulement pour faire une plaisanterie.*'

'No, no, Papa,' she tried to correct him, 'you mean to make yourself pleasant.'

But the Admiral knew well enough what he had said. He shrugged his shoulders. 'As you like, my dear,' he muttered, and I hid my feelings under a smile.

I must admit, however, that after a preliminary look round I was not very confident of obtaining any results at all. It seemed impossible to get near the slips. There were two cruisers moored to buoys just off them, and a string of boats doing guard duty. A sailing race among ourselves had only resulted in all our boats being turned back.

Then I had an idea. It happened that the Duke of Westminster had brought his yacht *Grianaig* to Kiel, and he had entered his motorboat *Ursula* for two of the regatta events. She was about the fastest craft of her kind afloat at the time and was attracting a great deal of attention from the German sailors who cheered whenever she was taken out for a trial run. It was this very general enthusiasm which gave me my idea.

That evening I invited the Duke to dine on board, and after dinner took him to my cabin. More than once I had proof of his good sportsmanship, and over our coffee I bluntly asked him to lend me the *Ursula* for an hour or two next morning.

'If you would do so,' I added, 'I would provide part of the crew.'

He stared and then smiled. 'The *Ursula* with some of your own men aboard? Rather a serious proposition, isn't it? I dare say it could be managed, but … do you think I might ask why you want her?'

It was my turn to smile. 'We want to see something they don't want us to see, and without your aid I'm afraid we never shall see it.'

'So it's like that? Right! Then what are the orders?'

I thanked him and explained:

I want you to try out the boat at full speed and over a particular course. I want her stopped at a given signal from one of my own men. Then I want the engines to go on strike for about ten minutes, and then – well, then I want them to start again.

'And during the ten minutes?' The Duke was grinning.

'Your people will be working like fury getting the engines right, and my people will be working like fury, doing something else.'

'Rule Britannia,' cried the Duke, and we shook hands.

And so early next morning one or two of my best men went on board the *Ursula*, and they bore little resemblance to the smart naval officers whom Prince Henry had so recently inspected. They looked like exceedingly competent engineers who spent all their time with ducal engines.

In a little while we were watching the beautiful boat speed out towards the open sea, make a wide circle and come roaring back up the harbour at full speed. The Germans had never seen her all out before, and they cheered madly as she passed them. So did our men, as I had turned the hands up and cheered ship. On she went at an incredible speed and burst right through the line of guard-boats. And then, well, it was a curious fact, but her engines broke down, and it must have been nearly ten minutes before they could be restarted. Even then not all was well, and I had the added satisfaction of seeing her safely towed back to her moorings by one of the guard boats.

The Germans were delighted to get such a close view of her, but they were hardly less delighted than I was, for one of the 'engineers' had secured the most perfect photographs of the slips and obtained all the information we wanted.

I should not like it to be thought that much of our information was obtained in wartime in this simple way, but the little story may serve to illustrate the unorthodox methods which so often had to be devised. Almost every week men were being asked by us to supply information, and in many cases it was impossible to provide them with more than the vaguest instructions. Often, indeed, we could not particularise the information that was wanted: something might seem to be wrong in this or that quarter, we would say, and we wanted to know what it was. And it was this general vagueness which as much as anything else led, as I shall shortly be telling, to the employment of men who in more normal times would have laughed at the idea that they could ever be of any conceivable use to a branch of our intelligence service.

Financiers, novelists, 'stupid sportsmen', insurance clerks, small tradesmen, to mention but a few; there was work which could only be done successfully by them and right well they did it. And here, I believe, was the secret of what successes we had. In my view a Director of Intelligence who attempts to keep himself informed about every detail of the work being done cannot hope to succeed. But if he so arranges his organisation that he knows at once to which of his colleagues he must go for the information he requires, then he may expect good results. Such a system, moreover, has the inestimable advantage of bringing out the best in everyone working under it, for the Head will not suggest every move: he will welcome, and, indeed, insist on ideas from his Staff. And so it was, from first to last, in the ID.

Information, however, also streamed in from those who were not in our employ, and this brings me to the second of my four points. Early in the war it became part of our policy to investigate every report, no matter from what source it might come. Here I still think that we were right, but it is a fact that with two or possibly three exceptions we never received information from 'outsiders' of any real value. A Dutch spy who was afterwards shot was brought to my notice by a stranger who telephoned late one night from a Bournemouth hotel. A young naval friend of mine, home on sick leave and recounting his experiences in the Red Sea, unwittingly helped to put us in possession of a much-wanted copy of the German Foreign Office cypher book. But in general outside information was useless. And yet much of it came from men who, you might have thought, were in exceptionally favourable positions to obtain news of enemy activities.

I well remember a visit early in 1916 from Sir Marcus Samuel, afterwards Lord Bearstead, a financial genius who before the war had interests in almost every part of the world. He came to see me at his own request, to repeat, with additional details which had just reached him, a story given in the previous year to Lord Fisher. From Mr (afterwards Sir Henry) Deterding he had learnt that the Germans were re-arming some of their newest ships with 17in guns. He admitted that he had met nobody who had actually seen these guns, but stated that recent reports from his own agents mentioned that the guns had been erected on temporary mountings and were not expected to last after an action of five or six hours. He added that Mr Colyn, the Dutch Minister of War in the last government, had also given him the same information. He was most insistent that I should not be sceptical about the matter, and earnestly hoped that we were re-arming our own ships to meet this new menace.

Now Sir Marcus was no busy body. He sincerely believed all that he had been told, and he was able to give me many additional and corroborative details which I need not enumerate here. I asked him if he believed that the *Blücher* was one of the ships particularly named as having been re-armed. Sir Marcus was convinced that it was, and then I was compelled to tell him that when the *Blücher* had sunk, she had her original armament on board.

And that, I suppose, may be cited as a typical example of well-intentioned information which had no basis in fact.

Luckily in the matter of information provided by our own men we were frequently able to tap more than one source. Sometimes there would be three or even four channels through which it might come, and, particularly towards the end of the war when almost every enemy code message was being intercepted, we knew soon enough whether a report was valuable or not. These intercepts, moreover, were of incalculable assistance to us in piecing together the various reports we were receiving.

As to the third and fourth points, illustrations of their importance will be scattered in some abundance through the chapters which follow, and here I need only stress the fact, not always remembered even by those who have written books about our work, that an Intelligence Division as such has no executive functions. In one of the war-books, for instance, I am made to issue an order stopping all cross-Channel traffic. Now it is quite true, as I shall show, that on two occasions such traffic was stopped, but it was only the Director of Operations who could properly issue the necessary order. Similarly when, as sometimes happened, it became advisable to give false information to the enemy, this would not be done on our own responsibility, but only in response to a request from, or after consultation with, those in charge of naval or military operations.

Incidentally, there is one other point of no little importance to a man who finds himself at the head of an Intelligence Division: it is advisable to remember that 'secret' information can very easily cease to be 'secret'. There were several occasions when I made myself highly unpopular by refusing to divulge information to those who, perhaps not unreasonably, considered that they ought to have been given it. But it is my experience that 'Silence where Possible' is about as good a motto as any intelligence officer can hope to adopt.

2

INTELLIGENCE IN WARTIME

Editor's note

This chapter takes the form of notes made by Hall for his talk in March 1936 at the Naval College in Greenwich to a large audience including members of the Foreign Office and representatives of all three services. Undoubtedly, this conference was part of the run-up to war three years later.

Spy systems are no good for the movements of ships as the time lag in getting information is too long for effective counter action to be taken. They are alright for acquiring knowledge of the enemy's material and resources and were found to be quite effective for this, vide results at the end of the war.

A very useful check on enemy's material is through insurance. Practically every private firm insures articles under manufacture and these insurances are reinsured through other insurance firms. This was the case with Germany where most of the reinsurances were effected in Switzerland. Sent out there a big man in insurance world who lived there for some months and through whom we secured lists of all war materiel reinsured; after a little practice, we could pretty well place what articles were being manufactured. This of course did not apply to government yards where no insurance was carried; we had to depend on agents for this latter work and they did well as we had a full list of all ships building.

. . . . .

Agents could also assist in giving information as to morale behind the line and were of assistance in showing where to put the screw on in the blockade.

. . . . .

Similarly, one used neutral countries largely for information. In one neutral country an English lady was married to one of the secretaries through whom all dispatches and telegrams to the head of the state passed. By this means we were able to read everything the ambassadors in the enemy country were saying to the head of their state and it might be mentioned that it was through this source that the first solid information of the coming collapse was received.

. . . . .

Information such as this cannot be trusted to the post. One had to devise means so that every time the copies were ready, they were passed by hand to another agent who brought them out of the country. The system lasted the whole war from 1915 onwards.

. . . . .

In the late war, movements of ships of the enemy were known through their use of wireless coupled with our ability to read their cyphers. Both decyphering and directional wireless were used to the full.

. . . . .

Cyphers are of course a subject which does not come in to this lecture but the methods of getting the original cypher books may be of interest and possible use.

. . . . .

Naval cypher ex *Magdeburg*.

. . . . .

Naval books and cyphers from enemy destroyers sunk in action and recovered by trawlers sent out for that purpose.

. . . . .

Zeppelins and their cyphers.

. . . . .

Submarines and their cyphers; use of corps of divers.

. . . . .

In no case was a cypher bought or stolen; by doing either of these, an astute enemy would be able to work off dud information on you.

. . . . .

We planted several cyphers on them with some success.

. . . . .

Rotterdam and the cypher. The role of Guy Locock.

. . . . .

Relieving pressure on the front by threatening a false invasion through the use of disinformation.

. . . . .

Use of newspapers; some examples.

. . . . .

The Daily Mail special editions; quote articles. Portions blacked out.

. . . . .

The Times and gold ship example; letters from a German agent sent in their code; result of this being that the Governor of the Bank of England wanted the gold.

. . . . .

Defence of convoys. Example; questionnaires taken off enemy agents in Norway. Imperative for them to ascertain how many subs we had working with our convoys. Paragraph in *The Times* re the sinking of a sub.

. . . . .

Extract from the sub sunk in the Straits of Dover confirmed by papers from the sub. Intercepted wireless messages quoted from *The Times*.

. . . . .

Zimmermann Telegram. Important that the enemy should believe that the Americans were responsible for its interception. Articles were placed in the American press praising the work of the American secret service.

. . . . .

Diplomatic cyphers. How acquired. Pipe line to Abadan raid; escape of Wassmuss; naval officer invalided; told me a story of an attack on the enemy's camp and how Wassmuss got away in his pyjamas on horse back, leaving his baggage.

. . . . .

Enquiries through India Office as to where the baggage was. Final discovery of the baggage in the cellars of the India Office.

. . . . .

Importance of never breaking line of enemy communication. Once across it, let it run on. Far safer than breaking it as then one has to find the new line and that is not so easy.

. . . . .

Example of Chakravaty in America; we read all his letters and let them go on. When America came into the war they, without warning, arrested Chak and we had great difficulty in tracing the new line of communication.

. . . . .

Combined work of agents and wireless intercepts; example of *Erri Berro* and tungsten.

. . . . .

Importance of covering one's tracks when making use of information in order to prevent the enemy from finding out how the information is obtained.

. . . . .

Example of the staff officer in Berlin and the reward offered by the Germans for his name.

. . . . .

Importance of patience in Intelligence Division work. Very often valuable information will come in which of itself would be of little use at the time but which if kept till the proper moment will have due effect.

Examples:

1. Publication of a list of names of 150 submarines' Commanding Officers' names, as having been captured or sunk. This could have been published very much earlier but would not have had the effect it did by keeping it. We published it at a time when German morale was on the decline and it was important to try and destroy their confidence in the success of their submarine campaign. This type of propaganda is invaluable as every family with a relative in a submarine knew it to be true.

2. Boxes dropped by *U35* in Cartagena harbour. One sent to me; the contents being sugar with tubes of anthrax in each cube. Knowledge of this was kept till it was time to undermine the position of Ratibor in Spain. Herschell told the King of Spain about it with the result that Ratibor left Spain.

The difficulties in handling information lie more in the direction of preventing its use in such a way as to hazard the line of information. An example of this is: the Foreign Secretary, when dealing with the Russians, handed the Soviet Ambassador a copy of his own telegram. The result was an entire change of system by the Russians and the destruction of the line of information.

. . . . .

Importance of orders being obeyed when handling secret letters. Example: the capture of a bag of mail from Constantinople when the messenger carrying it disobeyed his orders and went by steamer to Brindisi. The steamer stopped on route, the bag was thrown overboard, unweighted. The result was that names and addresses of agents became known and the whole organisation was destroyed, never to be rebuilt as we had let them down.

. . . . .

The only basis on which an organisation can be built up and maintained is by establishing confidence; once this has been shaken, the organisation will collapse. A classic example of this is when our agents were dealing with Talaat Pasha over the passage of the Straits to Constantinople. We could never reestablish contact nor would the men acting for us try again as they too had been let down. Better to pay too much than too little; pay even if you can't get at the time what you want. Once the other side know that you will carry out your word, there is always the chance that in the end you will get what you want.

. . . . .

Necessity for close reading of information and understanding what the natural deductions are.

. . . . .

Example of *Möwe* and *Bristol*.

. . . . .

Möwe sends in by ship all the captured masters; the captain of a cruiser interviews them and sends his report home by letter.

. . . . .

In our report is a statement that the last ship captured by *Möwe* was one carrying 6,000 tons of Welsh coal. *Möwe* took her in to the mouth of the Parana river. The Parana river emerges into the Atlantic Ocean through the Rio de la Plata, just north of Buenos Aires. From here to Germany is a distance of 11,844km. She coaled from her to the extent of 800 tons and then took her out and sank her.

. . . . .

The captain of the *Bristol* did not see the natural deduction to be drawn from this; that if *Möwe* were going to continue her cruise, she would have kept the coal ready for use. That she sank the collier after taking out what she wanted, showed that she was on her way home. In the result, the extended patrols which were at once ordered out, arrived on their patrols about eight hours too late and the *Möwe* got home safely. Had this information been cabled, there should have been little doubt but that we should have captured or sunk her.

. . . . .

Propaganda can be used for various purposes:

1. To deceive the enemy, as in the Falkland Islands. This is to lead him to take a certain course for which you are prepared or to try and relieve pressure from a position by getting him to move forces to resist a supposed movement on your part.

2. To undermine the morale of the enemy by attacking the morale of the non fighting population.

3. To induce neutral nations to either keep quiet or give assistance where and when required. A very good rule is 'if you don't help me, don't help him'.

4. To counter the war aims of the enemy by showing what would happen should they win. This had considerable effect in America.

. . . . .

The organisation of such propaganda falls naturally under two heads. The first head is propaganda which must be carried out through agencies in close touch with the higher command in order that HQ should not find itself embarassed by too zealous agents. The second head is civil propaganda which should be carried out under the control of the Cabinet. None know better than the MI how to run the former; luckily for us, there was the closest and most cordial relations between MI and ID, all through the war, so that we were able to practically pool our resources and our brains.

. . . . .

Most foreign countries have the highest respect for our leading newspapers and believe what they read in them. Particularly so in the case of *The Times*. One has to be very careful though if intending to use the latter that they shall in no way lose their prestige and whatever information you ask them to publish, must be well within the bounds of reason.

. . . . .

With the penny press of wide circulation one need not be so careful. They are quite accustomed to eating their words and digesting the result. Here then, an intelligence officer can have fairly free scope. If, as in the case of one paper, they will publish special editions for export, and have the relevant portion blacked out in the home edition, it becomes easy to arrange that both editions should be sent abroad. It would be difficult then for an enemy to believe that the information was not correct.

. . . . .

Again, a useful method of propaganda was found in the St James' club. Here met all the attachés and secretaries of neutral legations and embassies. One well known London figure was employed in the ID, much to many people's astonishment, for this purpose alone. A good lunch with the selected victim, a game of ecarte afterwards and the tongue strings were loosed. Little by little the desired information was passed on: the game stops. Away goes the secretary hot foot to his chief; a long cable with the valuable information passes over the wires that night which cable, if the organisation is as it was in the war, is fully understood by our own people. In practically every case when this system was used, the information reached the Germans in the neutral country. They, like good patriots, at once passed it on by wireless to Berlin and our listeners had the pleasure of passing up to me news that there was a leak somewhere and that such and such information had reached the enemy.

3

A PRIVATE CENSORSHIP

I have no doubt that somewhere in the Admiralty there is a document which sets forth in detail the precise duties assigned to the Director of Naval Intelligence. I have no doubt that some such list of instructions was available at the time of my coming to Whitehall. To this day, however, I have never, I believe, set eyes on any official instructions, and I cannot say that my ignorance about them ever caused me a moment's uneasiness or regret. It seems fairly clear to me now that I must repeatedly have exceeded my authority, and I probably annoyed a number of well-meaning gentlemen in responsible positions who saw no reason, merely because we were at war, to alter their views on procedure. There was a 'correct' way of doing things, and in their opinion failure to conform with traditional methods would inevitably bring chaos in its trail. But some of us new brooms did not see things in that light. For myself, I had had no experience of the politicians, and knew little about government departments. But I had not been many weeks at the Admiralty before I had come to the decision that if we were to get on with our job, there must be no slavish regard for peacetime precedents. There were certain things which in my view badly wanted doing, and I proposed to do them. There might be misunderstandings and even serious trouble, the worst that could happen to me would be to be relieved of my appointment and sent to sea.

And about the first thing that did happen was that I ran the risk of two years' imprisonment!

Largely as a result of my nefarious activities, however, steps were taken to form a new government department, the great value of whose work was never in question.

Now with the interception and deciphering of enemy wireless messages we had a most valuable method for obtaining information, but what of the equally important business of preventing the enemy from following our example? Here there were many methods which suggested themselves, and three of them were of immediate importance. In the first place there was the censorship of all telegrams, cables and wireless, the last-named an Admiralty job, and this was already in being as part of the general preparations for war. In the second place there was the search throughout Great Britain to make sure that there were no secret wireless installations in our midst. This, too, was being done, and in point of fact none of the slightest importance was ever found. In the third place there was the censorship of all incoming, outgoing and transit mails, and such a censorship had never been contemplated in peacetime, though it was now in process of formation.

On 9 October 1914, the Home Office had issued a statement about espionage in the course of which the postal censorship had been mentioned. After explaining very briefly that a Special Intelligence Department had been established some years before jointly by the Admiralty and the War Office, it had gone on to say that this department now had 'the assistance of the cable censorship', which, established originally to deal with correspondence with Germany and Austria, had been gradually extended as the necessary staff could be obtained so as to cover communications with those neutral countries through which correspondence might readily pass to Germany and Austria. Nevertheless I was soon convinced that it was imperative to enlarge very considerably the existing scope of the censorship and to press for its more rapid extension. Primarily, of course, this was not an Admiralty job, and yet it did not require much more than ordinary common sense to see that naval interests could be vitally concerned. Then some time in November, by a lucky side-wind, I received assistance from an unexpected quarter. One day a Member of Parliament called at the Admiralty with a report from a clerk who was working in the censorship. This clerk had formed the opinion, wrongly, as it turned out, that enemy messages were leaving the country in some abundance. At this same time his arguments seemed sound, and I was considerably impressed. At that time I readily admit that I was chiefly concerned with possible espionage, and had no clear idea as to what supremely valuable information of a very different kind might be forthcoming from the censorship, but in the ID we were not too happy at the general position, and I therefore made it my business to look closely into the matter.

And so for the first time I came into close contact with Colonel Cockerill. I have already spoken of the man who was so soon to become the Director of Special Intelligence at the War Office and of some of the multifarious duties which he was called on to superintend. Now I had the opportunity of studying at first hand the methods which he employed, methods, by the way, which I was soon to employ myself. Obviously it was impossible for one man, even for a man who in one capacity or another had been attached to the Department from its beginnings, to do much more than see that each of the many sections was properly functioning, but there was little that was being done in any of the branches which escaped his notice, and the postal censorship was no exception. And he was good enough to explain what was being done at Mount Pleasant, where in conjunction with the Post Office authorities, his men were doing their utmost to keep abreast with the ever-increasing foreign mails.

As I expected, however, the department had not yet been properly organised. This was hardly surprising, and Colonel Cockerill was in no sense to blame. It was necessary to create something out of nothing, and at the very beginning opposition from more than one quarter had had to be faced. The available staff remained lamentably small. On a recent visit to Mount Pleasant Colonel Cockerill admitted that he had found something like chaos: piles of letters awaiting special attention, cheques strewn about the floor, dozens of bags which had not yet been examined at all. I gave him the gist of the postal clerk's report, which, incidentally, had included the statement that of all the mass of stuff no more than about 5 per cent of the outgoing mails were being dealt with, and boldly suggested that we might be allowed to take a hand in the business.

He looked at me for a moment in silence. 'What exactly do you want?' he asked at last.

I must admit that I had not come to the War Office with any detailed plan in my pocket, but I was fairly certain that once I had secured Colonel Cockerill's interest and approval I should be able to lay my hands on the necessary money and staff. 'I want,' I told him, 'to make sure all the foreign mails are opened and that no secret message gets through. I want to see at work some organisation which will check the results of your men.'

'In other words a little private censorship of your own!'

'If you like to put it in that way, yes, with my own staff and at no expense to you.'

He nodded his head. I know now that he anticipated endless trouble with me, unless he could convince me fully that the whole of the services under his control would be organised throughout the war to suit naval as well as military needs. No word of his that morning was other than helpful, and I believe that our friendship, which lasts to this day, was born during our subsequent talk. Very briefly, however, he explained his difficulties, and they were undoubtedly serious. The special staff was small, and so far from any likelihood of there being any immediate increase, Cabinet ministers were already threatening the very existence of a postal censorship. Unfortunately political considerations had to be taken into account, and most of the Cabinet seemed to be definitely inimical to the section. There had been considerable trouble with the United States and other neutral countries, which were complaining, with some reason, of the long delays with their mails.

'Only a few days ago,' he told me, 'I was sent for by a Cabinet minister who in the presence of one of his colleagues said: "We propose to put an immediate end to all forms of civil censorship. What have you to say?"'

'But that would be suicidal!'

Colonel Cockerill waved a hand. 'The very word that I used myself, but foreign countries do make a habit of being disagreeable about such things, and one has to step very warily indeed. Troubles of this kind,' he continued, 'were fairly constant, and more than once the press had voiced the malcontents.' In particular, there had been repeated complaints that the ordinary commercial codes were no longer permitted to be used in foreign telegrams. To meet this complaint he was making arrangements whereby four of the best known codes would be allowed when, on 1 November 1914, permission was granted for these codes to be used, and a further three, including Bentley's and Broomhall's, were allowed to be used after 14 December. However, the whole position was one of the greatest delicacy, and it was necessary to move with extreme care.

'But about this proposed organisation of yours,' he finished:

if it would satisfy you to make a further examination of all the mails which pass through our hands say for two months, why then I would have no objection – provided, of course, that at the end of the experiment you report any weak spots you find in our organisation so that I may put them right. I shall expect you, too, to keep yours entirely secret.

Now this was a bigger decision than it might seem to be. Strictly speaking Colonel Cockerill had no authority to delegate to anybody outside his own department any part of the work for which he was responsible. Yet by allowing us to take a hand in the censorship work he was materially helping on that smooth collaboration between Admiralty and War Office without which the war could not have been won.

Naturally I agreed to his terms, and walked slowly back to my office.

That day, as usual, Colonel Browning, Lord Herschell and myself lunched together, and I broached to them what was really to be the first of those little shows of ours which continued on and off, with varying success, throughout the war. I explained the position, and asked for help. Our checking might have no very good results, but the experiment was going to be made, and made without delay.

'Freddie,' said I, 'what do you think? If I could find the money, could you find the staff?'

For a moment he stared blankly at me; then the look of excitement for which I had been hoping came into his face. 'But of course: Why, my dear fellow, I believe I could get you …'

'Yes?' I prompted, knowing very well what was in his mind. Here surely was fit work for the National Service League to undertake, but, could it be arranged?

'Two hundred fellows any use to you?' he asked at last. 'And offices to match?'

'Exactly what I want.'

'Right,' promised Freddie. 'In four days time they will be yours.' And he was as good as his word.

Meanwhile, however, there were the funds to be raised. It was necessary to keep the affair as quiet as possible, but obviously the First Lord would have to be seen, and that same afternoon I saw Mr Churchill in his room. I was not altogether satisfied, I told him with the censorship of letters, and wanted £1,600 for some extra work. With that sum I should be in a better position to judge what was going on. I was purposely vague. No details were offered, and none asked for. The money was immediately promised.

And within a very few days a new department was hard at work, with Lieutenant Colonel F.H. Browning in charge. There was a shortage of translators, and once or twice needless scares, but everybody worked hard, and within a week or two results were obtained which exceeded all expectations.

And yet not a single trace of espionage had been found!

Once again, however, we were in luck. The postal clerk had spoken of enemy messages leaving the country, and so they were, though they were not of the expected kind. They had no reference to matters of naval or military value, yet they were of no less importance. For they dealt in a more or less concealed manner with the methods whereby the enemy was obtaining, or hoped to obtain, supplies from overseas, and from our point of view such information was priceless, for unless we could produce irrefutable evidence that supplies found in this or that neutral ship were ultimately bound for enemy countries, our Prize Courts would refuse to condemn either cargo or ship, and the work of the navy in stopping such ships and bringing them in would be wasted. But here in these letters which our amateur staff were so diligently examining was just the evidence that was so badly needed. In a little while we were understanding how and where the Germans were ordering vast quantities of contraband stuff. It was a momentous discovery. Indeed, I do think it is not too much to say that our little censorship was the first real move in the new blockade.

Everything worked smoothly. The staff did not talk. And I do not think that any one of us was aware that the law was being quietly and systematically broken.

But it was too good to last.

Barely three weeks had passed before the blow fell. We made our first bad mistake. As it happened, it was also our last mistake in this particular business, though we were not to know it at the time. Late one afternoon I was told that Colonel Browning was on the telephone, and with the receiver to my ear I knew at once that something had gone horribly wrong. There was an unfamiliar note in his husky voice – a peculiar note compounded of indignation, disgust and a kind of scared solemnity. Yes, there was bad news. An office 'slip' had been left accidentally in one of the opened letters. And of course it had been left in the one letter that really mattered. A letter, said Freddie in his forthright way, addressed to the 'ruddiest of radicals', and a Member of Parliament to boot:

'But what exactly,' I asked, 'has he done?'

'Raised hell. Complained to McKenna. Threatened to ask the most awkward question in the House. Lord knows what he hasn't done. And I shouldn't be surprised,' he added, 'if McKenna doesn't raise hell as well.'

This warning reached me just in time. Before I left my office that evening a curt note had arrived from the Home Office. The Secretary of State for Home Affairs desired to see Captain Hall at eleven o'clock the next morning.

The situation was undoubtedly awkward, and as I walked across Whitehall the next morning I wondered what the day would bring forth. I had managed to have a few words on the telephone with Colonel Cockerill, but he had been too busy to tell me much more than that he, too, had been asked to come to the Home Office. His own position, of course, was rather different from mine in as much as he held the Home Secretary's warrant, whereas I, presumably, would be held to have been tampering with His Majesty's mail. At the same time some of the responsibility would be his. But I was not so much worried on his or my own account as irritated at the possibility that the good work which we had inaugurated might be held up owing to peacetime punctilio.

Until this morning I do not believe that I had ever been into a government office other than the Admiralty. At the time I knew little enough about politicians, and had not a notion how to deal with them. In my sea-going days it had never occurred to me that a time might come when I would have to deal with them. Mr McKenna himself I had met once or twice in his Admiralty days, but only on matters of the most ordinary routine. It would be a very different interview today. The fact remained that I had taken the law into my own hands. True, there had been no ill purpose on my mind, but would that be accounted sufficient excuse? Had the government yet realised the nature of its colossal task? I am afraid that in common with a number of my colleagues I was not too sanguine on the point. To most of us it seemed that except for Kitchener himself, and possibly the First Lord, no member of the Cabinet was yet prepared to forget his peace-time principles and fight with new and if necessary undemocratic weapons. I knew that if the Home Secretary ordered us to do so, we should have to close down our little show altogether, and in view of his recently delivered 'Business as Usual' speech could anything else be expected from him? Yet I was determined not to leave his room before putting my full case before him. At all costs he must be made to see the great importance of this new trade Intelligence Department which we were building up. It would not matter a jot who was put in charge of it, but that it should be closed down because a few neutral States might be threatening to make trouble was unthinkable.

There were, however, two points in my favour. In the first place there was the fine stand which Mr McKenna had made a year or two back in the matter of our naval programme, and it might well be that he could be persuaded to make a second stand now. In the second place I could depend on Colonel Cockerill's backing, for he had been the first to admit the good results of our experiment. Well, we should have to put up the best fight we could.

It was to be for me a peculiar but most valuable experience. I was shown straight into Mr McKenna's own room, and there he was standing in front of the fireplace, with his hands clutching the lapels of a long frock coat, a very solemn figure indeed. At his side stood the Permanent Secretary, equally solemn. Colonel Cockerill had already arrived, and I took my place beside him. We bowed. We stared at each other, and for a brief moment there was a funereal pause. And I remember wondering who was expected to speak first on such momentous occasions. But I was not long left in doubt, for after giving his lapels a little tug, the Home Secretary proceeded to address us in his best Parliamentary manner, as though indeed we had been [in] a public meeting. I cannot pretend to recall his exact words, but their gist remains very firmly in my memory.

'Commander Hall,' he began, I had been a captain for nine years and was in uniform at the time, but was addressed in this manner throughout the interview. 'I have sent for you because it has been brought to my notice that without my express authority you have dared to tamper with His Majesty's mails. Is this true?'

'Quite true, Mr Home Secretary.'

The two civilians became even more portentously solemn. An invisible wig seemed to be settling down on the Minister's head. Then he asked if had I realised the heinousness of my offence? Had it occurred to me that were he to do his duty, he would be obliged to take immediate steps to see that I was brought to trial, in which case on being found guilty I would go to prison for two years?

Had I not been so keen to make him understand the importance of our work, I think I would have laughed at that moment. It was just as if two senior boys had been summoned to the headmaster for breaking a rule to which nobody except himself paid any attention. But I did not laugh: I merely asked permission to explain, and taking that permission for granted, began to plead my cause to some purpose.

In a little while the atmosphere had changed altogether. The Permanent Secretary had gone, and Mr McKenna, Colonel Cockerill and myself were sitting at the same desk in the friendliest discussion. Indeed, within a bare half-hour that 'Business as Usual' speech had been forgotten, and I was remembering only the speaker's good work at the Admiralty. He was showing himself to be the big man whom I had hoped to find. Colonel Cockerill, too, had most loyally backed me by pointing out that although the Home Secretary's warrant applied only to himself, he had felt justified in accepting what temporary help he could get from outside until such time as his machinery was perfected.

'We have both been working towards the same end,' he said; 'and in my view it is essential that this organisation of Captain Hall's should continue until a new permanent department has been set up.'

'A War Trade Intelligence Department, in other words?'

'Exactly what is required,' said I, and in a little while had the Home Secretary's promise that he would see the Prime Minister on the matter without delay.

After which, events moved very quickly indeed, and, as it happened, victory came in a dramatic enough way.

Within twenty-four hours Mr Asquith had sent for me. He was cautious but friendly. His questions were admirably terse, and the first of them was sufficient to convince me that once he was satisfied that I myself had no ulterior motive, he would very definitely be on my side. And so it was. What exactly was it that I wanted, and why? I explained the position as we at the Admiralty saw it, and Mr Asquith nodded. He had, as I hoped, grasped the fact that all the older ideas about the blockade of an enemy country were disastrously out of date. The time had come for entirely new methods. Very well then, but what of the neutral countries? And what exact effect on the war could one hope for? And then, I remember, he put the only question that surprised me.

'How much,' he asked, 'do you suppose this suggested new department is likely to cost us?'

It was the one question which had never entered my head, and so much I was obliged to admit.

'But could you give me a rough estimate?'

'Half a million a year,' I hazarded, and to my great relief nothing more was said on the matter.

I left him with a roughly drawn plan of the proposed new department, and returned to the Admiralty a much happier man. For the Prime Minister himself I had conceived a very great liking, and although he had in no way committed himself, I was convinced that we had gained our point.

There followed a summons to attend a Cabinet meeting. I was to present myself at Downing Street at eleven o'clock.

I duly presented myself at the door of No. 10, a house to which I had never supposed I would be invited to enter. Was one expected to address the Cabinet? What was the procedure on such occasions? I did not know. I did not much care, for success seemed to be very near now. And then a curious thing happened. I suppose it happens to most people situated as I then was. Once inside this rather shabby old house I could not rid myself of the idea that I was only witnessing a strange kind of stage play. Things had suddenly become real. I was shown by a grave manservant into the Cabinet room, and I saw and heard the assembled statesmen in excited discussion, but I could not at first believe that I was actually in their presence. It was as if I were looking at an animated cartoon from the pages of *Punch*, and the ridiculous notion received support from the fact that nobody took the slightest notice of me.

And then as I took my stand by the door that led to Mr Asquith's private quarters, I realised that there was only one empty seat at the table, the big seat with arms halfway down the table in which the Prime Minister always sits.

So Mr Asquith had been detained. There was nothing to do but to stand there by the door and wait. I stood and waited, and the discussion grew louder. The Home Secretary and Mr Runciman, I remember, were in furious argument. Mr Churchill was studying some plans. Lord Kitchener seemed to be dreadfully tired.

Suddenly there was silence. I turned round to see the Prime Minister. He gave me a smile as he went to his seat. I wondered in what way the debate would proceed and at what precise point I would be asked to join in it. And then there happened one of those moments which one can never forget. I was not asked to speak. There was no debate. The Prime Minister still with a smile on his face, glanced round at his colleagues.

'Well, gentlemen,' said he, 'we have Captain Hall here, and I can see that you are all in agreement with his views. Good. Then we can take steps at once to form the new Department.'

And that was all. I do not remember leaving the room. I do not know whether I spoke to any of the ministers. But as I walked back to my office I knew as clearly as if I had been told so by Mr Asquith himself that in a little while the ID would be doing work far wider in scope than any Admiralty official even that day would have dared to prophesy.

I have only to add that in due course the War Trade Intelligence Department was set up, and a number of Freddie Browning's staff were taken into it.

5

THE CRUISE OF THE *SAYONARA*

This chapter has been seen by Commander Simon. Lord Sligo's name will not be given unless he approves. All official dispatches given here have been seen by Ralph Straus at the Admiralty by permission.

I pass on to you the curious story of the *Sayonara*.

The attention of the Admiralty was first directed to this American yacht in the third week of December 1914. A report, forwarded through Queenstown, referred to the arrival off the west coast of Ireland of the SY *Sayonara*, about 600 tons, flying the American flag. Considering the time of year this fact in itself was peculiar, and instructions were immediately forwarded to the coastguard vessels to keep her under observation. There was no reason, of course, why a rich American should not cruise in Irish waters if he chose, though he would do so at his own risk; but this was at a time when rumours were flying about that the Germans were using Irish ports for their submarines, and naturally there was more than a little suspicion.

Further enquiries, moreover, elicited some very odd facts. A few days previously the *Sayonara* had steamed into Queenstown Harbour. She had been boarded in the usual way, and the officer of the guard had then reported his suspicions about the owner, a Colonel McBride, who was on board. This man, it seemed, was an American citizen hailing from

Los Angeles, but he talked with a strong German accent and 'looked like a Hun'. On the other hand, the ship's papers had been found to be in order, and the captain, a 'wealthy Yankee' who made a 'hobby of navigation', had behaved in a perfectly correct manner. Both owner and captain had come ashore and met Vice Admiral Sir Charles Coke, then commanding on the coast of Ireland, and his staff. They had been invited to luncheon with them, and in the mess had shown anything but pro-British sentiments. There had, indeed, been more than one awkward moment. Nevertheless on explaining that they were only waiting for better weather to leave Irish waters for their annual winter cruise to Bermuda, the yacht had been permitted to depart.

The *Sayonara*, however, did not immediately leave Irish waters:

```
                                                    22.12.14
Coastguards to Admiralty.
Steam yacht flying American flag reported going towards
Killary Bay today. Defensible Queenstown informed.
```

At this time the weather undoubtedly was bad, and the yacht's captain had some excuse for not putting out to sea at once. So far, moreover, there had been nothing in the yacht's behaviour which called for any drastic step. Her owner might speak with a strong German accent, but he would not be the first American to do so; and in view of the already rather delicate relations between the United States and ourselves, it was considered undesirable to run the risk of any incident. A close watch, however, was maintained on the yacht's movements, and in particular Lieutenant Hicks of the *Safeguard*, one of the smaller vessels doing coastguard work, received orders to shadow her.

There was more definite news the next day. Apparently there was trouble with the yacht's engines:

23.12.14

```
Buncrana.¹ W. SS²to Admiralty.
Station officer left on board yacht at Killary. Boarded
yacht with police. Owner reported bound for Bermuda from
Queenstown; engine broken down. Named Sayonara, flying
American flag. This information has been forwarded to
Coast Guard station to await arrival of Safeguard.
```

And then one of our battleships, the *Cornwallis*, Captain F. le Mesurier, steamed into Killary Bay; it is a beautiful natural harbour, almost a fjord, and he was understandably inquisitive. Once again the yacht was boarded, and the officer in charge immediately raised his suspicions. According to him no American yacht had any business whatever in Irish waters at this time of the year, certainly not one owned by 'an obvious Hun'. Whereupon Captain le Mesurier himself went on board and subjected both owner and skipper to a prolonged cross-examination. He did more. On being told that the *Sayonara* was sheltering in the bay owing to boiler trouble, he had one of his own engineers put aboard, and this officer privately reported that he was not altogether satisfied with what he found. Other officers talked freely with the yacht's officers and crew – afterwards good-humouredly commenting on the curious ideas about discipline shown by the American sailors – and before disembarking made a full examination of the yacht. And they, too, were not wholly satisfied. But what, exactly, was wrong? Was the yacht's crew numerically larger than might have been expected? Yes, but this was not a British yacht. And the owner? He admitted that he had been educated in Austria, but was that to be held up against him? He was, he said, a rich man who loved the sea. Every year he spent as many months as he could

---

1   Buncrana is at the mouth of the River Crana in Donegal.

2   W. SS is War Signal Station.

on board his yacht, generally in European waters. This year the war had wrecked most of his plans, and the bad weather had added considerably to his troubles. And although he quite understood that the captain of a British man-of-war was obliged to take all possible precautions, was it really necessary that a citizen of a friendly neutral state should be treated in this rather high-handed way? They had scrutinised his papers, they had examined his yacht, and what had they found that was wrong? The usual courtesies were exchanged.

But the captain of the *Cornwallis* was in no mood for the usual courtesies. He was going to take no risks whatever. Nothing might be obviously wrong, but both he and his officers were agreed about one thing, and that was that proof was still lacking that everything was right.

And straightway he put the *Sayonara* under arrest.

Colonel McBride of Los Angeles became angry. He talked about the American Ambassador in London and about highly placed friends of his in the United States; the implications being that these gentlemen between them would have something to say which the British government would by no means be pleased to hear. And his language became even more strongly Teutonic. On the other hand, the skipper, a breezy fellow with any number of good yarns to tell, merely shrugged his shoulders and seemed to look on the whole business as an interesting war-time adventure which would make a fine story for the folks at home. Nor did he show any particular concern when he found his ship temporarily in the hands of the British navy.

Some of these details I did not learn at the time, for the official dispatch which reached the Admiralty during the next few days and was sent down in the usual way to the ID for remarks, were brief:

25.12.14

From Bunbeg[3]
To Admiralty

sent 12.30 a.m.
recd. 2 a.m.

I09 message 24th 11.55 p.m.
From Cornwallis
Following message sent by land wire begins:
On arrival at Killary found United States yacht *Sayonara*
New York Yacht Club. Papers were correct for clearance
from Queenstown for Bermuda on Dec. 21st. Yacht has
half Kilowatt Marconi W/T apparatus but no operator
apparently in crew's list. Examination by Engineer
officer does not confirm existing defects in engine. Have
requested vessel not to proceed for present.
Request instructions as to detaining or liberating.

Decypher 27.12.14.

From H.M.S. *Cornwallis*
To Admiralty   7.15.p.m.
Via Bunbeg W/T   recd. 8.30. a.m.
1800. My messages 24, 26 U.S.A. yacht *Sayonara*, Constable
informs me one reference given by acting owner Colonel
McBride is not genuine. Master anxious to proceed.
Request instructions as to what action should be taken.
(endorsed)
DID
Suggest telegraphing directions to ask owner for
explanation as to reason for arriving at Killary in view of
avowed intention of proceedings from Queenstown to Bermuda.
W.J. Evans

---

3   Bunbeg is a small seaside village in West Donegal.

28/12/14

```
NL

Suggest reply to Cornwallis: Safeguard has been detailed
to shadow yacht Sayonara, no further action considered
necessary at present.
                                     W.R. Hall, DID
                                       28.XII.14.
```

My own endorsement may read curiously in view of the police report, but, secretly I had arranged for other agents along the coast to keep the yacht under observation. Also it is as well to remember that although a suspected enemy agent behind prison bars can by himself do no further harm, he is well capable if left at liberty, even though aware that he is being watched, of making a little mistake; and little mistakes have been known to have big effects. Whether or not the *Sayonara* was an enemy spy ship she was being very closely watched and could do nothing without our being informed. Orders were therefore sent to Captain Le Mesurier to release the yacht forthwith.

It was then the gallant sailor's turn to be angry, and looking back on the whole affair I can well understand his indignation. In a further private report he implored the Admiralty to reconsider their decision, and it must be admitted that he made out a very good case.

First and foremost there was the owner, who not only spoke with the strongest German accent but could not always express himself in English. About the captain, he allowed, there could be no question: he was a good sailor who for some years had served in the American mercantile marine. And every member of the crew was undoubtedly American, but – what did a yacht of under 600 tons want with a crew of nearly fifty? And why amongst that fifty was none rated as a wireless operator? Then there were the yacht's engines. There had been a rambling explanation of boiler defect, but according to the examining officer there was nothing seriously wrong. Furthermore, no really satisfactory explanation had been given why so many months had elapsed without the *Sayonara* being able to leave European waters. Admittedly the weather at the moment was unusually bad, and for the last few weeks there had been frequent gales, but in September and October there had been fine spells, of which only a fool or a knave would have failed to take advantage. In short, there was no shadow of doubt in the minds of himself and his officers that the yacht was a German spy ship, and in view of the possibility of enemy submarines making use of various points along the coast as secret fuelling stations, he asked for permission to take the most drastic steps.

Permission was refused, and, judging from private letters, which I have seen, the disgusted officers in the *Cornwallis* came to hold no high opinion of the 'silly old gentlemen' at the Admiralty.

But there were others besides those officers who in a little while were finding that they 'could not understand what the Admiralty were doing'. The *Sayonara* had been released from custody but she did not immediately leave Irish waters. A telegram from military headquarters in Dublin to the War Office, and at once forwarded on to the Admiralty, informed us that at noon on 1 January the yacht had left Killary Bay and come to anchor the same evening in the neighbourhood of Westport. And there she stayed for some little time. Every day, moreover, a small party from the yacht would be put ashore. And once on land what did they do? They fraternised immediately with the Sinn Féiners; on one occasion, indeed, they were stoned by Irish loyalists and had to be rescued by the police. Then why was nothing being done? Letters poured in to the London office of the Navy League. It might be all very well in theory to give the dog a rope in the pious hope that sooner or later he would hang himself, but did nobody in England understand the alarming situation in the west of Ireland? Would it never be realised that quantities of empty petrol tins had been found, not in one or two isolated places, but regularly in dismantled huts and in caves along the entire coast? Would nobody in authority believe that the owner of this yacht who called himself McBride, though his real name was probably von und zu Somethingsteinkop, had actually been heard to speak German in an Irish hotel notorious for its anti-British clientele. And I must confess that more than one naval officer of high rank approached me on the matter and went away wholly dissatisfied with my declared policy of waiting and seeing.

Matters came to a head when the Marquess of Sligo (styled Lord Arthur Browne, of Westport House, County Mayo) arrived one morning at the Admiralty and insisted on seeing me. I had never met him, I knew nothing about him; but I understood soon enough that I was dealing with a patriot who had been thoroughly aroused and was in no mood to listen to any rules underlying intelligence work. Lord Sligo, indeed, was boiling with fury. He had rushed across from his house on the West Coast to make sure that I was personally made aware of the disgraceful state of affairs in his neighbourhood. He told me first about the petrol tins, but I was not greatly impressed by that piece of information, for it happened that the Germans were not using petrol in their submarines, a fact of which we had been fully aware from the beginning of the war, though we saw no reason to advertise our knowledge. His next piece of information, however, was more startling. With his own eyes he had seen the *Sayonara* planting mines in Westport Harbour.

'With my own eyes,' he repeated, 'and if the whole damned lot of them are not arrested and interned at once …'

'But we can't intern American nationals.'

Lord Sligo waved an angry hand. 'Captain Hall,' said he in very solemn tones, 'I am no scaremonger. I would not have crossed the Channel to tell you some cock-and-bull story. These fellows may be Yankees, but they're in the pay of the Germans, and I'm not going to sit still and watch them planting mines under my very nose. And I warn you that if steps are not taken immediately, I shall raise the matter in the House of Lords. Oh, I know, I know, what you're thinking: we mustn't run the least risk of offending our American friends. There must be no unnecessary publicity and all the rest of it. But there's been enough dilly-dallying. Look at this scoundrel Casement: I don't return to Ireland until I know that something has been done.'

'Very well,' said I, 'then I will show you a confidential report which I have just received from one of our best men.'

It was not my usual practice to show any such reports to casual visitors, but I had my own reasons for allowing this particular one to be seen by Lord Sligo. It was a detailed account of a visit paid to the *Sayonara* in the vicinity of Westport by a 'stupid Irish yokel' who had rowed himself out in a boat with vegetables to sell, and expressed wonder and delight at the 'pretty ship' and been allowed to come aboard and see her interior beauties. Apparently he had made himself agreeable to both officers and crew, though this was hardly surprising in view of his statement to them that to him and all his relations the United States had long stood for the Promised Land. Already various members of his family had migrated, and he was only waiting for the war to end to follow their example.

And what had this 'stupid yokel' to report? That the *Sayonara* was a genuine American yacht, wholly unarmed. That there was no reason to suppose that the owner was not the American citizen he represented himself to be. That the Germans could be pretty good fools, but that they were hardly likely to employ as a spy a man who could hardly speak English and 'resembled an overfed Kaiser'. That the captain was a 100 per cent American impartially contemptuous towards all European nations, whether at war or not. That the crew, Americans all, were an illiterate lot with little interest in anything except their wages, their chewing gum and their food. That the owner had certainly met some of the local Sinn Féiners, but that such suspicions as these meetings might have aroused could in a measure be discounted by the fact that the Sinn Féiner of whom Colonel McBride had seen most was a man of his own name, a man, indeed, who claimed him as a relation. That while there still remained some ground for suspicion, the *Sayonara* had been kept under the closest observation from the moment when her presence in Irish waters had become known to the authorities, and beyond the fairly frequent visits ashore, nothing had occurred at or near Westport which could suggest hidden activities.

'Yes, yes, yes,' cried Lord Sligo, 'that's all very well, but I tell you I saw them at work. I saw the mines dropped overboard, and nothing will persuade me I didn't. And if you still refuse ...'

'But, Lord Sligo, nobody except yourself has suggested that mines have been laid within miles of Westport Bay. There has been no report of any casualty. Nothing. I really think you must be mistaken.'

At that my visitor flared up. If this was the way that the Admiralty was being run, we should deserve to lose the war. He would go at once to Lord Fisher. He would beard Mr Churchill. And if their replies were as unsatisfactory as mine, nothing should muzzle him in the House of Lords. They might shut him up in the Tower if they liked, but he knew where his real duty lay.

I saw that the time had come to give him a little more information.

'I should like,' I interrupted, 'to tell you something about the *Sayonara* which is not to be found in the report you have just seen. I must only ask for your assurance that the information will in no circumstances whatever go beyond yourself.'

He stared. 'Yes, of course, but ... You have my promise,' he finished stiffly.

So I told him the truth, or rather a small part of the truth, and I have rarely seen anybody quite so astonished.

'You need have no fear of the *Sayonara* so long as she stays in Irish waters. Her "owner" is a major in our army who has won the DSO. The "American" captain is a naval lieutenant who served with me in the *Queen Mary*. Every one of the yacht's crew is now serving in the British Navy. And my last visitor before yourself this morning,' I finished, 'was the yacht's courier – a very good man – who, I expect, crossed by the same boat as yourself.'

But I did not tell Lord Sligo in what circumstances the *Sayonara* had been commissioned, or what work she had already succeeded in doing, or what curious duty she was still hoping to perform. The full story, indeed, is only now told in print for the first time. It was never known to more than three or four people, and even the man who first suggested the use of an American yacht in Irish waters and found us the *Sayonara* did not know the full extent of her commission.

So far as I was concerned the whole business may be said to have begun in the United States, where in September 1914, the German Ambassador and his staff were making their first big endeavour to win over American opinion to their cause. Reports from various quarters showed us along what lines their propaganda was being directed. 'We are most likely to find friends,' ran one of Bernstorff's cabled messages, 'if we give freedom to oppressed peoples, such as the Poles, the Finns and the Irish. What American opinion is afraid of, so far as it is against us, is in the event of our victory, an excessive extension of our frontiers over areas where foreign languages are spoken. The decisive point seems to me to lie in the question whether any prospect of an understanding with England is now in view, or must we prepare ourselves for a life and death struggle? If so, I recommend falling in with Irish wishes, provided there are really Irishmen who are prepared to help us. The formation of an Irish Legion from Irish prisoners of war would be a grand idea if only it could be carried out.'

Now the 'Irish wishes' mentioned in this cable referred in particular to Sir Roger Casement's proposals, and five weeks later Bernstorff was informed that Casement himself had arrived in Berlin. A further cable from Zimmermann, then Under Secretary at the German Foreign Office, dispatched on 6 November contained a message from Casement to Judge Cohalan in New York. It referred to the fact that we had discovered the identity of Karl Lody, the spy – he had been executed the day before – and were 'greatly alarmed' at the state of affairs in Ireland. We were 'taking all costs' to find out precisely why Casement himself had gone to Germany. Furthermore, it was suggested that a 'native-born American citizen' should be sent without delay to Ireland, to act as liaison officer between Casement and his friends.

That we were highly interested in Casement's movements at this time was true, though the 'at all costs' was an addition which personal vanity must have prompted. We knew that at the beginning of the war he had gone to New York and put himself into touch with Irish Republicans like John Devoy and Judge Cohalan and with von Papen and Boy-ed at the German Embassy. We knew that he had sailed in October for Norway (narrowly escaping capture on the voyage), where he had complained of a plot against his life in which the British Ministry was supposed to have been concerned. Very wisely von Papen refused to make capital out of this alleged 'British atrocity'. And we knew soon enough about that proposed Irish Legion. We were only doubtful about the exact manner and date of Casement's attempt to return to Ireland. It seemed likely, however, that it would not be long delayed; in point of fact a Danish steamer was commissioned for the purpose two months later, though at the last moment the whole expedition was postponed. I was much exercised in my mind as to what steps to take when I received a visit from Sir Basil Thomson, who came to discuss the Irish situation in general and in particular the difficulty of obtaining reliable information about possible 'beds' for German submarines off the west coast.

In the course of our conversation he told me that Mr Shirley Benn, MP for Plymouth (who is now Sir Arthur Shirley Benn Bart, KBE), had come to him with a proposition, which he thought might just be practicable. It was that an American yacht be hired and some of our own people put aboard. A cruise along the west coast could then be arranged, and in that way we might obtain the necessary knowledge.

It was a good idea, but could such a yacht be obtained? It would have to be fairly large. There would be trouble with the American authorities if they discovered what we were doing under cover of their flag, but need they ever discover? And then another plan suggested itself. With such a yacht acting secretly under our orders useful information from the west coast might be forthcoming, but might it not also be possible by its use to alter in some way the manner of Casement's projected return to Ireland? He would come, I presumed, either in a German submarine or in a neutral steamer. Could there not then be some masquerade or impersonation on the part of our yacht? This was not the moment to go into details, but would not some such scheme be workable – with the right man in command? And immediately I knew who the man must be.

Tentatively I put forward my proposal. Sir Basil Thomson agreed that it seemed good, though he foresaw many difficulties. Yet before he left me that morning to return to Scotland Yard, we had worked out in rough outline the scheme which was ultimately adopted. We had decided that if the right kind of yacht could be found she must have a genuine American for captain and a 'German-speaking' owner. Sir Basil thought that he could find a man to play the part of owner; I had promised to produce an American captain.

And after that things happened very quickly indeed.

Mr Shirley Benn immediately got in touch with Mr P.J. Hannon, then Secretary of the Navy League, and together they went to the Thames Yacht Club to examine the shipping news. They found two American yachts which might be suitable. One of these, the *Sayonara*, belonged to Mr Anthony Drexel, the well-known American sportsman who was then in England, and through the good offices of Mr Almeric Paget, MP, (afterwards Lord Queensborough, GBE), a meeting between the three men was arranged. Mr Drexel's first inclination was to refuse all co-operation. The proposal, he thought, was illegal; he might very easily get into trouble with his own government. But he was heart and soul with the Allies, and on Mr Benn's suggestion that the yacht be chartered in the ordinary way to himself or his nominee, he agreed, believing that Benn himself would be sailing in her to this second plan. It had first been intended that Mr Benn should sail in the yacht, but we were of the opinion that he might be recognised by some Irish ex-MP when the *Sayonara* put into port, and it was thought undesirable for him to accompany the party. It was a fine gesture of friendship, which was nonetheless appreciated because we were not in a position publicly to recognise it.

As soon as I heard that the *Sayonara,* then lying at Southampton, had been secured, I took the necessary steps to get hold of my 'American'.

Now it happened that when the *Queen Mary* had been commissioned, her RNR lieutenant had been a man named Simon. He had not remained long with us; early in 1914 he had transferred to the Royal Navy, but it had been long enough for me to learn what an efficient officer he was. His previous career had been unusual. In 1910 he had sailed (as navigator) under the American flag in the Airship *America*, the only Englishman amongst the crew, at the first attempt to cross the Atlantic. Afterwards he had served with the Cunard Line and amongst his many accomplishments was a quite extraordinary flair for imitating American modes of speech. The lower deck, I had discovered, invariably called him the Yank. And I was never in doubt as to his being the one man for the present purpose. At this time he was in the *Russell*, but a request for his services brought him speedily in mufti to the Admiralty.

The interview in my office was short.

'Can you become an American for me?' I asked.

'Sure, Cap,' said he with a grin, and from that moment Lieutenant F.M. Symon, RN changed into Captain Simon, late of the USMM.

I then explained more or less what we had in view. By this time our plans had matured. Only those actually concerned were to know the truth about the *Sayonara*. To the world, which of course would include all British authorities on sea and land, she would be what she pretended to be – an American yacht on her winter cruise. A letter would be given to Simon showing his credentials and real identity, but it was not to be used except in an emergency. As to Casement, it now seemed probable from our information that he would be brought to a point off the Irish coast by a German submarine and landed by means of some yacht or small steamer. We hoped, through our interception of German wireless, to be in a position to know when and where the rendezvous would be,

and at a given signal the *Sayonara* would play her part. For this purpose
a wireless apparatus was to be secretly installed (to take the place of the
one which had been officially dismantled), and arms were to be hidden.
The Admiral commanding at Portsmouth had been requested to provide
fifty naval ratings 'for special service', and so soon as the yacht was ready
to sail, she would be joined by her 'German-American owner', who
would know what to do when the submarine came. Meanwhile there
was much work to be done along the west coast, and amongst her crew
would be a man well-qualified to play courier between the yacht and
myself at the Admiralty.

Later that day I took Simon with me to Scotland Yard to discuss
details with Sir Basil Thomson, and it must be put to his credit that he
entirely deceived so shrewd an observer as BT.

Two days later he was in Southampton, preparing for what I suppose
may be called the first of the hush-hush ships.

There remained only the 'owner', and here Sir Basil Thomson was as
successful as I had been with the captain. Major Wilfred Russell Howell
was a very remarkable man. He had had a most varied and dramatic
career in many parts of the world. His father had been Chamberlain to
the Pope, and he himself had been born in France. He was, of course,
a Roman Catholic, and so, as it happened, were the other two officers
detailed for service in the Sayonara – a fact which was not without its
amusing side, for in my request to the Admiral at Portsmouth I had, for
fairly obvious reasons, stressed the importance of choosing only men
belonging to the Church of England for the Irish cruise. Howell had
been educated at the Feldkirch College in Austria and for a while in
Scotland; but afterwards he had rarely remained in his own country
for more than a few months at a time. By profession he was a railway
engineer, but soon enough he had shown other and more picturesque
activities. In 1898 he had served in the Mendi Rising at Sierra Leone
raising a volunteer corps and being the first volunteer to receive the
DSO. Two years later he had fought, and been severely wounded, in the

South African campaign. At a later date he had worked in Rhodesia and Mashonaland, and then gone as general manager to one of the Havana railways. He was a keen sportsman who had travelled extensively in four out of five continents, and not always only for pleasure. He could speak several languages, German like a native, his own, as it happened, least well. He was, indeed, a typically fine soldier of fortune, and in view of his many qualifications had been attached for some time to one of our branches of intelligence.

This was the man who with the necessary passports and papers in his dispatch case joined Captain Simon at Southampton on the morning of Tuesday 15 December.

The cruise did not begin too auspiciously. There was no trouble with the Portsmouth authorities, for I had sent a telegram two days previously, saying that the American yacht should be given permission to pass through Spithead without being boarded. But three of the *Sayonara's* own crew had had to be kept on, and two of them complained that they had not signed on for this kind of work. In Southampton Simon had allowed them to think that the yacht was bound for Bermuda, but in the English Channel he explained the real nature of the cruise, and there were demands to be put ashore. Time, however, was short, and there was nothing to be done but to hoist the White Ensign for a few minutes while the Articles of War were read. On the other hand the bo'sun and all the naval ratings were very willing to play their novel parts. Once smuggled aboard they were served with American kit and their uniforms hidden. A short lecture from Simon on the Yankee traits which it would be well for them to assume without delay was listened to with the greatest attention, and not even the prospect of a leaveless Christmas would dismay them. Unfortunately the yacht was almost in sight of the Irish coast when it was discovered that the wireless operator did not understand the Marconi apparatus which had been installed – it differed from that in general use in the navy – and as it was most important to reach the west coast within the next twelve hours. There was nothing to do but to put in at Queenstown and endeavour to find another operator.

This was done, and, as I have already related, suspicions were immediately aroused. A guard was placed on the yacht, and Simon and Howell were requested to come on shore. They did so, and were received with every formality by Admiral Coke surrounded by his entire staff. I gather that the 'two Americans' acquitted themselves well, but all suspicions were not allayed, and Simon felt that the moment had come to show the letter. He asked to see Admiral Coke alone, and his request was granted.

'Have I your word of honour that you will divulge nothing of what I am about to say?'

The words were bold, but Simon was still playing his part.

There was a moment's hesitation, and then the Admiral gave his word.

My letter was handed to him, and the Admiral may be excused for admitting that he was damned. He showed, indeed, signs of annoyance – he considered that he ought to have been told officially about the *Sayonara* – but he soon saw the joke of the thing, and on learning why the yacht had put into Queenstown, promised to find a wireless operator.

'I've got the very boy for you here, but how? I know. I'll send him aboard tonight to effect repairs. When you get him, well, you'd better up anchor and clear out. You'll have to provide him with clothes, as I can't send him to join you without rousing suspicion. There'll be the hell of a row when they find out that you've shanghaied him, but it's the only way.' And still chuckling, he insisted on the 'two Americans' lunching in the mess with him.

'But, mind you,' he ordered, 'you've got to pull our legs!'

I would give much to have been present at that luncheon. From all accounts it must have been exceedingly funny. Every officer present, except the Admiral, retained the deepest suspicions of the guests, and yet were forced to remain polite even when, as soon happened, Simon in his most boisterous mid-western way gave it as his opinion that this time we had probably bitten off more than we could chew. 'You Britishers,' he told them with considerable gusto, 'have no conception of what the German Navy is like, but I've had opportunities of seeing it, and I know. We've got a great admiration in my country for you, but, if you'll excuse my saying so, the Germans are a fine people, and I can only hope you'll be able to patch up some kind of peace with them before it's too late.' And 'Colonel McBride', battling nobly with his English, did not hesitate to support him. As an American, of course, he was strictly impartial in 'this regrettable business', but he was bound to say that his very considerable knowledge of Germany and her inexhaustible resources, had led him to believe that only by a miracle could she be defeated. He was sorry to appear so pessimistic in such a company, but his lengthy sojourns in Germany and Austria …

A distinctly uncomfortable meal for the staff, but a very valuable meal for Simon and the others, for all this play-acting had the desired effect. Henceforth those on board the *Sayonara* were so 'chivvied' by the British authorities that the 'bad boys' came to them like flies to a treacle pot, and they were able to meet almost everybody along the coast who was working against us. It was in order that suspicions might not always be allayed that 'Colonel McBride of Los Angeles' on one occasion deliberately gave a reference which was not genuine. He got his name, by the way, in the most haphazard manner. As the *Sayonara* entered Queenstown Harbour a launch came alongside and demanded the name of the owner. It was the one little point in the preparations which had been forgotten. On the spur of the moment Simon shouted out 'Colonel McBride', and henceforth Howell was obliged to stick to the name. Curiously enough the most prominent Sinn Féiner at that time in Westport was a McBride, and he really did try to claim relationship with the major, who on his side did all that he could to discover common ancestors.

A list of suspects had been provided, and every single one of them was interviewed. Within a month, indeed, Simon and Howell were able to sum up the situation on the west coast in no uncertain manner. It was largely due to their efforts that right on to the Irish Rebellion of 1916 we were able to keep watch on the most disloyal elements with comparatively few men. Every few days Petty Officer Hayward would cross Ireland with dispatches and return with what instructions it was possible to give. At one time some rumour of an oil dump would have to be traced to its source, at another some subterranean cave would have to be searched for arms. Every harbour between Achill and the Shannon into which it was possible for a vessel of the *Sayonara*'s draft to enter, was visited, and the work was never suspended for more than an hour or two, except when the yacht was put under arrest by my old friend Mesurier in the *Cornwallis*.

It says much for Simon and those who were with him in the *Sayonara* that neither the men's uniforms nor the hidden arms were ever discovered, in spite of the most thorough search. And when at a later date I told le Mesurier the truth, he could hardly bring himself to believe me. 'You mean to say that hard-boiled Yankee skipper was a British officer? That pork butcher of a Hun a British major? ...'

All the while, however, they were waiting to receive news of Casement, and for some time I was in almost daily expectation of being able to send it to them. A few extracts from my letters to Simon at this time may be of interest. 'Lieutenant Hicks of the *Safeguard*,' I wrote on 18 December 'will bring you this. He has orders to shadow you. Let him know your W/T wavelength and get his. I have told him to be very suspicious of you and your doings, and I think he will play his part all right.'

He did. He remained exceedingly suspicious all the while. And so did his first officer, who was not in the know. It was this officer who discovered that the Sayonara was carrying wireless. As it happened, Lieutenant Hicks was on shore at the time. The moon was shining brightly over Killary Bay, and first officer caught sight of the single wire serial on board the *Sayonara* which was always down in the daytime.

Immediately he went on board, and not only uttered threats in good naval language but informed the *Cornwallis* of his discovery. This concealed aerial and the fact that no wireless operator was to be found in the crew's list did as much as anything else to convince those in the *Cornwallis* that the *Sayonara* was an enemy ship and the Admiralty people a lot of incompetent asses.

Within a week I was congratulating him on the full reports which he had been able to send me, and suggesting that if he could get round inside Achill Island and find safe anchorage he would probably be on the danger spot. The weather made this impossible, but frequent visits ashore kept us in touch with every move. A few days later I was asking him to trace some oil which had apparently been landed at Cashel pier. Then at the beginning of the New Year I was able to give him news of Casement.

'It is anticipated,' I wrote on 4 January:

> that Casement will arrive in the Danish steamer *Mjölnir* of Copenhagen, 500 tons. She is due to leave Christiansand on the 9th, and should be off the west coast of Ireland between the 13th and 15th of January. With Casement will be Adler Christiansen, age 24, height 6ft, strongly made, clean-shaven, fair hair, gap in front teeth, wears thick double-breasted greatcoat and soft dark hat. Speaks English fluently but with Norwegian-American accent. Says he is a naturalised American but retains Norwegian nationality in Norway. He is wanted by the police in New York. I hope to get his rendezvous, but it is doubtful; but I feel that you are just about at the best place round the coast from Cashel to Achill.

On the 8th I wrote again: 'It is possible that Casement will be accompanied by six to eight German officers. If you get track of his vessel near a fort, do not hesitate to wire *en clair* – using your own call-sign at the end, to identify message. There will probably be ships in the vicinity to assist if necessary, but this will depend where steamer goes. Personally I do not think it likely that a Danish steamer will put into a west coast port: more likely she will wear British ensign and change her name. Casement is supposed to have a large sum of money (£20,000) with him, but this may be all bluff.'

Unfortunately, so far as we were concerned, there came a sudden change in Casement's plans. The Germans had discovered that all Ireland was not so anti-British as the traitor and American messages had led them to think. Obviously a great deal of preparatory work would have to be done before Casement and his German officers could put themselves at the head of an Irish rising with any hope of success. And for a while Casement himself disappeared from our view. 'We have lost track of Casement,' I was obliged to admit on 19 January, 'and unless you hear to the contrary, make arrangements to be back in time to turn over the yacht by the day named in the charter.' At the time of writing I was waiting for a report from Ireland, but when it came it only confirmed our belief that the German authorities had decided that any attempt at revolt in Ireland would be premature. The *Mjölnir* sailed from Christiansand, but without her Irish passenger. There was nothing to be done but to bring the *Sayonara* back to England.

This, however, was not too easily accomplished within the day named in the charter. The yacht was in Cashel Bay at the time, and gale succeeded gale. Coal supplies were running short, and it became necessary to take a chance. One morning the wind dropped though the Atlantic was still in an angry mood. But the anchor was weighed, and 'I shall never forget,' Simon told me, 'the swell that was running outside the harbour. There was one patch marked 14 fathoms on the chart, on which the sea was actually breaking! But we decided to stick to it, and twelve hours later were battling against another gale. We ran up channel before a snorting south-wester and arrived off Portsmouth about ten o'clock at night – to be greeted with a blaze of searchlights and a shot across our bows!'

Next morning ex-Colonel McBride of Los Angeles and the navy ratings were landed at Portsmouth, and the *Sayonara*, manned only by Simon, his two officers and three permanent members of the crew, returned safely to Southampton, once again an American yacht.

She had not taken Casement, but, as I shall be showing in a later chapter, she had not sailed in vain.

On 1 July, however, she was commissioned as HMY *Sayonara*, No. 035, for service as an armed vessel, and she remained in commission until 11 October 1918. Her captain, too, lived to do other good work during the war. He commanded more than one of our 'Q' ships. But that is another story, with which I had nothing to do.

6

A LITTLE 'INFORMATION' FOR THE ENEMY

I have mentioned the four chief points in intelligence work, but there is a fifth which in wartime is hardly less important. The assimilation and careful analysis of information never ceases, but such work may be called defensive, and it occasionally becomes advisable to take the offensive. In other words, information is deliberately given to the enemy, not always so scrupulously accurate as it might be, though not, I hasten to add, always entirely false. For although in a majority of such cases the information purposely conveyed to the enemy is false, it is sometimes useful to arrange for them to be told the truth, or at any rate a part of the truth.

In this connection I remember once engineering a little affair, the telling of which might show me in a singularly unfavourable and even traitorous light, were the story not told in its entirety.

It is not generally known, I think, that on one occasion after 19 August 1916 the whole of the Grand Fleet put to sea.

The events of 19 August 1916, when both British and German fleets were operating for the last time together in the North Sea, had led to very definite changes in naval policy on both sides. Von Scheer's new system of fleet reconnaissance had been shown to be unworkable, and Admiral Jellicoe's recommendations for a change in naval tactics were extensive.

True, there was no battle or even skirmish, and the cruise was remarkably short; but put to sea it did, and the Germans were well aware of the fact. Indeed they had been prepared for such a move, for precise information to this effect had reached them some days beforehand. For this, however, no German agent had been responsible: the information had come from the Intelligence Division itself!

It may sound a little curious, but that was the truth. I told the Germans that on such and such a day the Grand Fleet would come out, and it did. What is more curious, it came out for the sake of one man.

Now it will be remembered that the work in Room 40 was kept so secret that hardly a dozen men outside its door knew even of its existence. But from the beginning the command-in-chief had been kept fully informed, and both Jellicoe and Beatty saw every intercepted message which could be of any use to them. The time came, indeed, when I was in almost daily communication with Admiral Beatty, and I was often his guest up at Rosyth. It was during one of these visits that I asked him if it would be possible for him to help me in particularly difficult matter. Certain information was urgently required from Germany itself. I need not particularise what it was, but for some time all our efforts to obtain it had failed. There was one man, however – he was not an Englishman, though a good friend to this country – who might be in a position to obtain it if he could furnish the Germans with proofs that he had exceptional means of access to our most secret councils.

'Suppose,' I suggested to Admiral Beatty, after explaining the general position, 'that he were able to tell them that the Grand Fleet would put to sea on a particular date, would it be possible for this to be done without risk?'

'You mean the briefest of cruises?'

'Only sufficiently long to show that my man's information was good.'

'Well,' said the commander-in-chief after a short pause, 'I see no reason why not. Yes, go ahead.'

And so it happened that on a date settled between us the Grand Fleet put to sea, and returned. What the Germans thought about the singular manoeuvre I do not know, but they were more than satisfied with their informant, who, when he had obtained their confidence, was able to give us the particular information that we wanted.

In general, however, the giving of information, whether true or false, to the enemy, was not a matter for the ID alone. We would work in the closest co-operation with other departments, in particular with the military authorities, and more often than not, I should say, at their suggestion. And this brings me to the man who of all others, I suppose, best deserves the thanks of his country for rounding up the nests of German spies in England at the beginning of the war.

I first made the acquaintance of Major, now Lieutenant Colonel Drake in October, 1914, and this was the beginning of a long and intimate collaboration in intelligence work which lasted until he went on special service to GHQ in France. After passing the Staff College and holding Staff appointment at the War Office, Drake had left the army early in 1912 in order to perfect our counter-espionage service. Before the war he had been responsible for the arrest of men like Gunner Parrott, the publican Gould at Chatham, the notorious Armgaard Graves and others. These arrests had been effected in such a way that the Germans never suspected the existence of any defensive service of the kind, with the result that they were lulled into a false sense of security, and when war broke out Drake with the help of Scotland Yard was able to capture the whole of their spy service in Great Britain. As Colonel Nicolai admits in his book, the Germans could then get no information whatever from this country; they did not even know, he adds, that our Expeditionary Force had sailed, until it hit them.

At the time of our first meeting Drake had had a piece of bad luck. He had barely affected the arrest of Karl Lody before he was rushed to hospital to be operated on for appendicitis, and it was owing to his enforced absence that Lody's trial was conducted, not as he wished and intended, in camera, but in public by a full-dress court martial. As a result the Germans heard of the spy's arrest almost immediately, just the one thing which Drake wished to prevent, for he had devised an ingenious method for conveying false information to the enemy which depended on their not knowing which of their agents had been caught. Soon enough, however, all espionage trials were conducted in camera, and, what was equally important from his point of view, the name of the arrested spies were no longer published. Drake's scheme was put into execution, and worked exceedingly well. In this, so far as naval affairs were concerned, I was of course able to collaborate, and between us I think we succeeded in carrying out one of the first principles of war, that of mystifying and misleading the enemy.

About the first occasion when Drake gave me proof of his ingenuity was in his cool use of that most official of all official publications, the *London Gazette*. Already in those early days the German submarines were beginning to be a menace to the safety of shipping in the Channel, and it became necessary to devise measures which would at once put them off the scent and, if possible, provide opportunities for their destruction. For this purpose information was conveyed to the Germans that owing to the submarine menace transports were no longer being sent to France from Dover or Folkestone but from other ports further west, such as Weymouth or Brixham, which had been specially selected owing to the improbability of their use as bases being suspected by the enemy. To lend colour to this piece of information the *London Gazette* announced the appointment of several of Drake's personal friends, much to their consternation, as Embarkation Officers, Class 2. No ports, of course, were mentioned, but on conveying a copy of the *Gazette* to the German Intelligence Services, stress was laid by our correspondent that his 'man in the War Office' had told him where these Embarkation Officers were to function. When this information had been given time to soak in, details would be sent about an embarkation which was shortly to take place. It would not be true to say that this always had the desired effect, but on more than one occasion a German submarine slipped round to Weymouth or some other Western port to find a vessel waiting for her which bore no resemblance whatever to the transports she had expected to see.

This, however, was only one of many such schemes which were evolved in Drake's fertile brain. Another one came early in 1915, and although my own part in it was small, I give a brief account of it here because it illustrates very well the close co-operation between naval and military departments in a matter which was of purely naval interest.

In the middle of January we received many reports about the feverish activity at Kiel and Wilhelmshaven, and Beatty's battlecruiser squadron remained at its base instead of proceeding north for gunnery practice. On the 17th the Admiral was ordered to support a reconnaissance by the Harwich flotilla in the neighbourhood of the Heligoland Bight. For the next few days, however, there were little signs of any impending attack, though two Zeppelins dropped bombs in and around Yarmouth. What exactly was afoot remained obscure, it is not too clear even today, but we were fairly certain that the enemy sortie would extend at least as far as the Dogger Bank, and this is what did happen on the night of the 23rd. There is no need for me to describe in any detail the events of the next day. The action soon resolved itself into 'a plain stern chase', in the course of which the *Blücher* was sunk. Unfortunately Beatty's flagship, the now historic *Lion*, had been struck twice within a few minutes about 10 a.m. and three times again in the course of the next hour – the last hit being serious enough to render her port engine useless. Hence she could steam no more than 15 knots and she was forced to drop astern. Her speed was further reduced in the early afternoon when her starboard engine was giving trouble, and at 3.30 it was necessary for her to be taken in tow.

All available protection was now needed for her, for a destroyer attack was hourly expected. The next morning she was still 100 miles from her base and in an area in which German submarines were known to be operating. But there was no attack, and at a very early hour on the 26th the *Lion* was safely berthed in the Firth.

Only temporary repairs, however, could be affected at Rosyth, and it became necessary to move her south to one of the yards at the mouth of the Tyne. And so, some days later, with a strong escort of destroyers, she steamed down at night under her own power.

So far she had been lucky. There had been no attack. On the other hand enemy submarines had been watching, and at least one of them remained in British waters, apparently waiting for the chance to complete her destruction. In the well-guarded Forth this had not been possible, but she was followed south, and a day or two later we received information that a submarine had taken up a position at the mouth of the river, with the obvious intention of getting the battlecruiser when she left the yard.

That same day Drake was in my office, and I gave him this rather worrying piece of news.

'Submerged, I suppose, all day, and up at night?'

'More or less,' I agreed. The trouble is that they'll probably work in reliefs.'

'And how long are the repairs likely to take?'

'About a fortnight. They're working on her day and night, of course.'

'I see. No longer than that?' He was silent for a moment or two. 'That's pretty quick, isn't it?' he went on. 'Quicker than I should have expected for a ship that had to be towed in. Possibly quicker than the Germans expect? I wonder … How would it be,' he broke off, 'to let the Germans think she's much more seriously damaged than she is?'

'An excellent idea!'

'Then I think it could be managed. Give me a little time. I've got an idea.'

He rushed away but was back again within a few hours. 'DID,' said he:

I remember when I was at the Staff College being shown a secret book of photographs which the Japanese government had presented to the Admiralty. These photographs showed the damage done to the various Russian ships at the battle of Tsushima. Could I have a look at that book?

I had not a notion what was in his mind, but I sent for the book and, against all the rules and regulations, allowed him to take it away with him. The next morning he came back with it and asked to be put in touch with the Naval Construction Department, then under Tennyson d'Eyncourt. I sent him there with one of my staff, and as a result of his visit the German submarine at the mouth of the Tyne returned peacefully to its base.

What Drake had done was this. In the secret book were a number of photographs of the *Petropavlovsk*. These he had shown to the technical experts in the Naval Construction Department, and asked to have any details pointed out to him which might date the ill-fated Russian ship. On being told the reason for his request, the experts had been delighted to help, and, armed with his new knowledge Drake had gone to a firm of photographers who by the next morning had produced some half-dozen fakes with which we could have deceived most people outside the Naval Construction Department. To all appearances they showed a *Lion* most appallingly damaged, a *Lion* which by nothing less than a miracle could be got ready for sea within two months. They were, indeed, masterly examples of the photographer's art, and the Germans were hardly to be blamed for being deceived by them.

Deceived they certainly were. The photographs were sent over to Germany with a carefully composed letter which had ostensibly been written by one of their cleverest agents. The fact that this gentleman was then safely under lock and key and would shortly be shot remained unknown to them until some time after his execution. As for the letter itself, it explained how these most interesting photographs had been purloined from the Admiralty and must be returned without delay and before their loss had been discovered. It pointed out the impossibility of the *Lion* being moved from the yards for many weeks. And in view of the importance of the photographs, it asked for a good sum of money.

The photographs were duly returned. Obviously they had been most thoroughly examined, for I remember seeing them with German fingerprints distinctly visible. The money was paid, and the submarine was hurriedly withdrawn.

Decidedly a neat little job, and not without its lesson, for it shows how important a sharp memory can be in intelligence work. Had Drake not remembered a book of photographs seen years before, the *Lion* might not have survived to take her part in the Battle of Jutland.

In another affair of the kind the ladies, as it happened, played their part, though it was by no means the part which they had desired to play.

At the end of March, 1915, there had been held at Berne an international conference of Socialist women. It had been called by Clara Zetkin of the German Social Democratic party, and twenty-eight delegates, including Miss Margaret Bondfield, had attended. It was of no importance, and little enough trouble had been caused by its meetings, but it was generally felt in this country that this was not the time when any such conference could serve a useful purpose. Considerable surprise was therefore expressed when, only a day or two after this conference had issued its report, the announcement was made that an international congress of women was to be held at the end of April at The Hague, to discuss the principles of a peace settlement.

Surprise, however, soon gave place to disapproval. Many of those who had been most prominent in the women's suffrage movement publicly disassociated themselves from anything of the kind. Yet there were others, some of them very well known, who announced their intention of going to The Hague. For myself, I fully agreed with Mrs Pankhurst who, in spite of the fact that one of her daughters had identified herself with the congress, declared on the first week of April that those who talked of going were well meaning, but were 'being made use of by other people'. In the ID we had a fairly good idea of what the German peace terms at this time would be, and such information about the congress itself as we had been able to obtain suggested that the German case would be much more strongly presented than that of the Allies. Neither French nor Russian women, we knew, would be allowed to attend, and it would be just as well, we thought, if, like them, the British delegates were to be conspicuous by their absence. At that time, I think, no definite action had been taken, but it became known that the Admiralty viewed the conference with no friendly eye.

It must have been in the second week in April that the Home Secretary asked me to see him, and this time I saw Mr McKenna alone. He was obviously embarrassed. Some extremely important ladies, it seemed, wished to attend the congress. In all 150 had applied to him for permits. That number was of course far too high to be considered, in view of the fact that the congress was to be held at a place so near to the seat of war, where, it was known, enemy agents were making great efforts to obtain fragments of intelligence as to the movement of ships and men. After consultation with the Foreign Office, however, he had agreed to issue twenty-four permits to those who represented the chief of the women's organisations and sections of thought. 'I have, in fact, committed myself,' he finished, 'and now I learn that your people object.'

I agreed that the position was awkward, but I would not commit myself.

'They have my word, you see, that the necessary passports will be forthcoming; but if your objection continues, I shall be put into the difficult position of not being able to fulfil it.'

I was thinking hard. Nothing that the Home Secretary had told me in any way altered my views about the congress itself; on the other hand I could sympathise with him in what was an exceedingly trying position. 'Then it is really only a matter of passports.' I said, 'so far as you are concerned? Well, Mr Home Secretary, in view of what you have said, we will certainly raise no further objection to their being issued.'

He seemed greatly relieved, and we parted with mutual good wishes.

Nevertheless no more than four of the British ladies attended The Hague congress, and these four, who had crossed over to Holland some time previously in order to assist in the preliminary arrangements, were not in a position to take any prominent part in the proceedings. On 22 April the whole of the twenty-four names were published, and every member of the British delegation had been given her passport as promised. Unfortunately its main body met with a sudden and wholly unforeseen difficulty: they were unable to find a ship to take them to Holland. They waited with what patience they could right on until the 28th when the congress opened under the presidency of Miss Jane Addams, Chicago's most wonderful woman, but there was no ship for them.

The reason was simple. From the 21st all traffic between this country and Holland had been stopped, and, with the exception of a single steamer which carried mails and nothing else, no crossings were permitted until 3 May.

With three exceptions none took place. On the 29th, the Netherlands Minister called at the Foreign Office and complained that three merchant vessels had arrived in British ports from Rotterdam and were unloading their cargoes 'in spite of the supposed interruption of all traffic, while ships of regular Dutch lines were not able to run'. Of these ships one was British and two Norwegian, and he protested strongly against what appeared to be an unfair discrimination against Dutch ship-owners. Actually, however, these three ships had left in ignorance of the suspension order, and no discrimination had been shown.

It is hardly to be wondered at that Mr McKenna was angry. Questions were asked in the House of Commons, and the only possible reply roused ribald laughter. The ladies had officially been permitted to go, and now they were being held up in this rather ridiculous way. There followed one of those interdepartmental 'breezes' which all the good will in the world cannot always prevent. Why, demanded the Home Secretary, had this drastic step been taken without the express authority of the Cabinet? Nobody seemed to know. And who was responsible? There seemed to be an idea that the Director of Naval Intelligence might know something about it. Unfortunately that gentleman had taken to his bed. In point of fact I was down with a bad attack of influenza at the time, though at least one of my colleagues still maintains that the influenza on this occasion was of the diplomatic variety. Very well then, said the Home Secretary, now thoroughly roused, as, indeed, most of us would have been in his place, he would give himself the pleasure of seeing Lord Fisher; and round to the Admiralty he came.

Now the actual order for suspension had been telephoned about two o'clock in the afternoon to the customs authorities in London and to the Senior Naval Officer at Harwich. It came from Claude Serocold, who was well aware of my views on the matter, though not of course until after consultation with the First Sea Lord. Lord Fisher, however, was unwilling to tell the Home Secretary why the order had been given on this particular day, and suggested that Lord Kitchener was the man to see. Whereupon Mr McKenna paid another visit, this time to the Secretary of State for War, only to learn that the stoppage had been carried out at the Admiralty's request.

There followed considerable ructions which lasted until the following evening. Quite a number of important officials were convinced that somebody ought to be 'for it', though nobody cared to fix the blame on to any one man. Serocold, I am afraid, spent an unhappy twenty-four hours, for to a great extent his hands were tied and he could not give more than the vaguest explanations. Finally, however, it was agreed between the various parties who considered themselves aggrieved that nothing should be done until the Prime Minister returned from Newcastle, where he had been delivering his historic speech on munitions. And, luckily for us, on his return south Mr Asquith was told the full story and immediately endorsed our action.

But was the traffic stopped, you ask, merely to prevent a few well-meaning ladies from raising their voices at The Hague? No, there were other and weightier reasons, though it suited our book to keep them to ourselves and to blame the congress for the dislocation of traffic.

In point of fact it was a combined move on the part of the naval and military authorities, and it was intended to serve the double purpose of misleading the Germans in Belgium and of 'screening' our impending attack on the Dardanelles.

For some little time, we knew, German agents had been reporting to Berlin elaborate preparations on our part for an attack in great strength on the Belgian coast. Actually any such plan had been abandoned at the end of January. Measures were taken, however, to keep the enemy well supplied with reports of this nature. 'Evidence' was even provided to show that an early invasion of Schleswig was contemplated. And these measures were not without their results. There came movements of German troops which were only explicable on the assumption that they were expecting some such move on our part. What, then, would they think of a sudden stoppage of all traffic between this country and Holland? At the least it would increase their uncertainty and might possibly ease the situation in France, a matter of the greatest importance in view of the recent decision, so strongly opposed by Sir John French, to send certain troops then in France to the Dardanelles. It will be remembered, too, that the landing of the Dardanelles Expeditionary Force had been fixed for 25 April.

To what precise extent the Germans were led astray by the stoppage of traffic I would not care to say, but amusing confirmation of their anxiety at the time reached us a little later in the year. It happened that Drake, who was still busily engaged in playing his part as a German spy, found himself short of material and conceived the notion of having a little invasion of Schleswig all on his own. He therefore sent the Germans a detailed account of a large, but wholly imaginary fleet of flat-bottomed boats and tugs which were being assembled at Hull. With these a landing was to be effected on or near to the island of Sylt, the object being to draw off German troops from France.

In due course the German reply reached him. They were obliged for his letter, but they had had enough of this Schleswig invasion business in April, when they had been put to a great deal of trouble for nothing. They refused to believe in an invasion. Naively enough, however, they demanded to be kept fully informed about the Hull fleet and the intended attack upon Sylt, a fact which caused Drake to stand firmly and boldly on his dignity. If, he wrote back, his service was not worth employing, they had better say so plainly and be done with him. But what was he to think? Did they consider his Sylt information nonsense, or didn't they? He must really ask for a definite answer. If they no longer believed in him, well, there were other quarters where his wholly exceptional opportunities for acquiring information would be appreciated.

This letter had the desired effect. A humble apology was forthcoming together with a further pleasantly large sum of money, in the spending of which, by the way, I played my part. Visitors to my room at the Admiralty may remember a lordly fender. Drake's friends may also remember seeing him in a most comfortable car. Both were paid for by the Germans.

They did, however, boggle at one of Drake's requests. In a subsequent letter he enlarged on the excellence of his information and the terrible risks which he was obliged to run to obtain it. Would it not therefore be fitting for him to be given a decoration, which he could hand on to his children in the event, unfortunately most likely, of his dying for the Fatherland? But this was too much. The reply came that this was hardly the time for such things, which was a sad disappointment to me and, indeed, to several of Drake's closest friends, for I do believe that if he had succeeded in getting some German order, he would not have hesitated to wear it.

Incidentally, I ought to mention the fact that as a result of his efforts to disturb the peace of Schleswig, many hours were wasted by German second-line troops, who were set to dig elaborate trenches for miles along the coast.

In his role of German spy, Drake enjoyed a good enough innings, but the time soon came, as we knew that it must, for him to shut up that particular shop. The necessity, however, of conveying false information to the enemy remained, and other methods had to be devised. I have already mentioned supposedly indiscreet people like Ralph Nevill who could be trusted to pass on to the right quarters such 'secret' information as we wished the Germans to hear. For some little time we had been preparing an intelligence move designed to suggest to the Germans a forthcoming invasion of north Belgium. The general scheme was not dissimilar from Drake's 'invasion of Sylt', but it was being conceived on a much larger scale. Indeed, the initial steps taken by the ID were being as carefully arranged as if the War Council had actually decided upon the operation. Our campaign had been launched in the usual way by the judicious spreading of vague rumours. In the St James's Club there was much whispering, and I remember that on one memorable occasion at a lunch-party to which several important citizens of neutral states had been invited, I was myself as 'indiscreet' as to incur a private rebuke afterwards from a distinguished politician.

It then became advisable to make use of the Secret Emergency War Code. Wireless messages were sent to various stations. They could not of course be understood by the recipients, but all were duly intercepted and decyphered by the Germans. Messages were even sent to some of our ships telling them what they would shortly be required to do, a fact which led to some little confusion, for their officers, too, had no means of reading this strange cypher.

At first not too many details were given, but in a little while the enemy had been furnished with sufficient hints to understand fairly well our intentions. The expedition was to leave these shores in three separate groups – one from Harwich, another from Dover, and a third, the largest, from the mouth of the Thames, where it seemed, a fleet of monitors and tugs was rapidly being concentrated.

There remained only the choice of date when this second Expeditionary Force was to embark, and here we took advantage of the trouble in the channel which I have mentioned above. Traffic was being stopped, as it assuredly would have been stopped in the event of the supposed fleet of monitors putting to sea.

One other method which was used for conveying false information to the enemy may be mentioned here. It was based on the fact that although the Germans placed little enough reliance on most of the British newspapers, they were very ready to pay the closest attention, at any rate in the earlier part of the war, to anything which appeared in those controlled by Lord Northcliffe. Time and again an inconspicuous item of 'news' was inserted at the request of the Naval or Military authorities in *The Times* or the *Daily Mail*, generally in confirmation of 'information' already conveyed to the enemy by other means.

There was for instance the case of the *Kronprinz Wilhelm*, an entire failure I am sorry to say, so far as the ID was concerned. This armed merchantman had been operating with considerable success against our ships off the Brazilian coast, and we did our best to get her into some position where we could be sure of her capture. This was in the spring of 1915 while Drake was still playing his part as a German agent, and he invented a cousin, married to an Englishwoman, who was working as an Admiralty messenger. Several letters were sent to the Germans giving more or less accurate information about our ships in the Pacific, and when the trap had been sufficiently baited, we invented a mail-steamer which was bringing to England a large consignment of Gold from the Cape. This vessel, the Germans were informed, had been ordered to proceed from Lagos to a point considerably westwards (and not too far from the area in which the *Kronprinz* was known to be) where she was to be met by an escort. Unfortunately on the day fixed for our mail-steamer to leave Lagos the *Kronprinz* came to the end of her tether. She had been seriously damaged when ramming one of our ships, and she was short of both coal and provisions. She ran for a United States port, and was lucky to make it.

How far our little plan would have succeeded had she steamed eastwards to meet our imaginary ship it is difficult to say. It had failed, but that was not to say that our own part in the affair was at an end. In failure or success, there must be no loose strings about. The Germans must continue to believe that even though they had been unable to make use of it, the information given them had been good. For this reason our mail-steamer from the Cape was not allowed to disappear at once, and at the right moment a short paragraph appeared in the city page of *The Times*. 'Considerable satisfaction,' this ran, 'is felt in financial circles at the safe arrival in London of a large consignment of gold from the Cape, as there was some danger of it being captured by a German raider.'

That morning I was at my office at 8.30, but there was a man there before me. Standing in front of my fire was the sturdy figure of the Governor of the Bank of England.

I could not imagine what had brought Lord Cunliffe at such an hour to Admiralty.

'Where's that damned gold?' he growled abruptly.

There was nothing to be done but to tell him the whole story, which he thoroughly enjoyed. Henceforth, indeed, we were very good friends, and to the end of his days he would ask me in a theatrical whisper whether I had any more secret consignments of gold for him.

A much more elaborate scheme, however, in which the *Daily Mail* played its part, was set afoot in the following year. There were times during the war when the *Daily Mail* became extremely unpopular; there were times when, in my view, its attacks on the Admiralty were unjustified; but there was never a moment when its editor, Tom Marlowe, the best type of patriot, was not actuated by the best of motives. And when asked to help in this particular scheme by preparing a special edition of the *Daily Mail* for German consumption, he was even angry at my asking what the cost would be.

This was in the autumn of 1916, which, it will be remembered, was not a good time for us. Intensive submarine warfare was being resumed, the Zeppelins were coming over in fleets, our armies in France were being held up, food was becoming short and there were political troubles. At the beginning of September, moreover, we in the Admiralty were given good proof, though it was kept from the public, of the real seriousness of the submarine menace.

On the 3rd we learnt that a German submarine was at work between Beachy Head and Cap d'Antifer. All east and west traffic was immediately held up, and every available destroyer set to hunt down the invader. Fresh reports showed that one if not two other submarines were operating nearer Dover; and during the next seven days we had the unhappy experience of learning that two, or at most three, German submarines in the Channel, though hunted by thirteen destroyers and seven Q-ships, with nearly 100 destroyers and torpedo boats and more than 400 armed auxiliaries on the watch, could not only sink some thirty British and neutral vessels but could return to their base without damage.

Now it happened that in the previous month a request had come from the Military authorities for another 'naval diversion'. A wily paragraph appeared in the *Daily Mail* on which its special correspondent may be congratulated. And it well served its purpose, for the Germans did precisely what we had expected them to do. They believed Mr Wilson, and sent in reports to men who must have been waiting to hear something of the kind.

Our scheme, indeed, was successful, but it was almost too successful. For although it led the Germans to mass troops along the Belgian coast, which was what we wanted as they had had to be moved up from France, it also led to the worst invasion scare which we had in this country. Our trenches along the east coast were hurriedly manned:

local commandants worked for twenty-four hours a day; orders for the evacuation of residents in all towns and villages near the sea were on the point of being issued. And why? Because our agents in France had reported to the military authorities the German move north which in their view could have only one meaning: they intended an invasion of England. And although our friends in the War Office immediately informed us of this massing of German troops, I could not at once take the responsibility of saying that it was due only to the move which we had taken ourselves.

And that is the true story of the great invasion scare.

1325789
0643741
3690677
4336797
6120995
3258096
3146615
3407632
3680863
1009753
3456789

7

LORD FISHER AND MR CHURCHILL

In this chapter, it is suggested that the naval attack of 18 March was made as result of the von Usedom telegram. This chapter is to be seen by Lord Reading, Captain Crease, Griffin Eady and George Lambert.

It was barely three weeks after my appointment in Whitehall that Lord Fisher returned to the Admiralty and immediately made his presence felt.

Previously I had seldom come into personal contact with him, but he had known my family for years. My father had sat with him on the first Torpedo Committee, and at a later date had been asked to go as his commander in the *Inflexible*. For various reasons the invitation had been declined, but it has an interest for me because it was while the *Inflexible* was commissioning at Portsmouth that, as a very small boy, I was introduced to him by my father. My first official meeting with him had been in December 1905 when he had sent for me to say that he had decided to appoint me Inspecting Captain of the proposed Mechanical Training Establishments. These new schools were intended to turn stokers into mechanics and boys into engine-room artificers. They had to be built up from almost nothing at all. 'Ask for anything you like,' said Lord Fisher on this occasion, 'except money. I want all they'll give me of that for the Fleet. But you know what's got to be done, so do it.'

And that was the Fisher of those earlier days, a magnetic figure. One did know what had got to be done, and in one way or another managed to do it. Luckily these training schools prospered, and when we met once again in the *Queen Mary* a week or so before war was declared, he was good enough to speak well of my work as a 'trainer'.

So far, indeed, as I was concerned, his return to the Admiralty was very welcome. That there would be ructions and upheavals was to be expected but that did not matter so long as the things which so badly wanted doing were done. In point of fact there were many changes in personnel within the first few days of the new regime and I cannot say that the work of the departments did not suffer for a while on that account. From one hour to the next you could never be quite sure whether a man would be found at his old post. But in those first few weeks at any rate the new First Sea Lord in spite of his age, he was seventy-four, remained the tireless and exacting and magnetic figure whom we had long known and admired.

As we have seen, he was brought in too late to alert the disaster at Coronel, but his sending of the two battlecruisers to the Falklands and their subsequent success did more than anything else at the time to revive the navy's good spirits. And we at the Admiralty hoped that once again the real executive control would be in the proper hands: the hands of the First Sea Lord and not in those of a civilian First Lord.

This, I hope, does not sound too ungracious as coming from a man to a former chief to whom he owes much. I liked Mr Churchill: liked him very much. I admired his genius and dash. He was always approachable and always ready to back you up as far as he possibly could. His energy and capacity for work were almost frightening. Notes and memoranda on every conceivable subject could stream forth from his room at all hours of the day and night. What was worse, he would demand information which would ordinarily and properly have gone only to the First Sea Lord or Chief of Staff, a fact which more than once led to some confusion and an unmerited word of rebuke.

On 6 November 1914, to give a rather ludicrous instance, I took up to the Chief of Staff a report of great importance, which we had received from Belgium. The Germans, the report informed us, had rushed between 200 and 300 mines to Zeebrugge. As it happened, however, the word 'mines' had not been used, for our Zeebrugge agent had his own way of describing things. To him anything which did not move or float on the sea's surface was 'submarine'. This peculiarity of his was of course known to the ID, and so much I had explained to the Chief of Staff, though the explanation was hardly necessary. The Germans could not have sent that large number of submarines to Zeebrugge or anywhere else for the simple reason (very generally known at the Admiralty) that they did not possess them. Mr Churchill, however, had recently sent me a written order that any information from Belgium was to be sent to him as and when received, and so a copy of this message was sent to the First Lord's room. And next day the rebuke came:

```
NID
                                    November 7, 1914
With reference to your report of yesterday, apparently
attaching credence to a statement that from 100 to 200
small submarines have been manufactured secretly in
Germany, have you considered how many trained officers
and personnel this important flotilla would require?
What evidence is there at your disposal to show that the
Germans have trained this number of submarine captains
and officers? I have always understood that their flotilla
of submarines before the war did not exceed 27. The
function of the Intelligence Division is not merely
to collect and pass on the Munchausen tales of spies
and untrustworthy agents, but carefully to sift and
scrutinise the intelligences they receive, and in putting
it forward to indicate this degree of probability which
attaches to it.
```

But I took the view that unless the First Lord was himself doing the executive work, the information in this report could not have been of use to him, and so forwarded it, as ordered, without comment.

It would be unfair, however, to imagine him wasting valuable hours on small points outside his province. He had both courage and vision, a brilliant man if ever there was one. But he had the defects of his great qualities: he was essentially a one-man show. It was not in his nature to allow anybody except himself to be the executive authority when any action of importance had to be taken. Even in matters of the most extreme technicality he would insist on an elaborate presentation of his own views, and his powers of argument were so extraordinary that again and again tired Admiralty officials were hypnotised – I can think of no better word – into accepting opinions which differed vastly from those they normally held.

Once, I remember, I was sent for by Mr Churchill very late at night. He wished to discuss some point or other with me at once. To be candid, I have not the slightest recollection what it was: I only know that his views and mine were diametrically opposed. We argued at some length. I knew I was right, but Mr Churchill was determined to bring me round to his point of view, and he continued his argument in the most brilliant fashion. It was long after midnight and I was dreadfully tired, but nothing seemed to tire the First Lord. He continued to talk, and I distinctly recall the odd feeling that although it would be wholly against my will, I should in a very short while be agreeing with everything that he said. But a bit of me still rebelled, and, recalling the incident of the broken shard in Kipling's *Kim*, I began to mutter to myself: 'My name is Hall, my name is Hall …'

Suddenly he broke off to look frowningly at me. 'What's that you're muttering to yourself?' he demanded.

'I'm, saying,' I told him, 'that my name is Hall because if I listen to you much longer I shall be convinced that it's Brown.'

'Then you don't agree with what I've been saying?' He was laughing heartily.

'First Lord,' said I, 'I don't agree with one word of it, but I can't argue with you. I've not had the training.'

So the matter was dropped, and I went to bed.

Unfortunately, Mr Churchill showed no inclination to resign the executive command on Fisher's arrival, and there speedily came an atmosphere of friction which could not altogether be hidden and was not wholly due to a difference of opinion about the campaign in the Dardanelles. Undoubtedly the idea of this campaign was not at first unattractive to the new First Sea Lord, provided that there could be an element of surprise about it, and it was not only loyalty to Mr Churchill which caused him to show all his old energy in the matter of assimilating the necessary details for its furtherance. Right on to the time when it became clear to every one of us that only a campaign on the hugest scale, impossible in view of the military situation on the western front, could affect the forcing of the Dardanelles, Lord Fisher was eagerly exploring every approach to the problem. As I shall relate, there came a day when his eagerness for immediate action equalled Mr Churchill's. It was from him that I received orders to buy up all the lighters and tugs to be found in Greek waters, and he was able to put me on to the one man, Richard Grech, who was best suited for that unusual job. His investigations, moreover, were not confined to purely naval questions, and he more than once surprised me by his extensive knowledge of little-known political history.

Early one morning there came down to me a typical and not too polite note, scrawled in the usual green pencil, and in view of what happened later, it is not without interest: 'Tell W.R. Hall,' it was addressed to Captain Crease, his naval secretary:

to find out from the Foreign Office by 11 a.m. where Fitzmaurice is, he was last at Sofia, and what his orders are. He is now the most important person in the Eastern Theatre of the War but unfortunately this is not realised. I told Sir Edward Grey over and over again he could get the Bulgarians to march on Constantinople from Dedeagach if he was authorised to give them Kavalla, Salonica and Macedonia, and therefore dish the Greeks who are poltroons and sneaks.

It was some satisfaction to me to be able to tell him that I had been in regular communications with Fitzmaurice who was working hard for us. There was no man alive who knew more about Turco-Germanic relations than did Gerald Fitzmaurice. For years he had been attached to our embassy at Constantinople, and nothing had moved in that city of intrigue without his knowing every detail. Unluckily in pre-war days our government in their eagerness to placate Germany had listened to Berlin. Representations were made through the usual polite channels that Fitzmaurice's activities were by no means helping the cause of Anglo-German friendship. If he could be recalled …

It was so easily done but it is a fair speculation to wonder whether history would not have been considerably altered in the Near East, had this most exceptional man been permitted to retain his post. I for one have no doubt that we should have been given ample warning of that secret treaty between Germany and the Turks. We knew nothing until many months after the information the treaty contained could have profitably been made use of, when we were able to decypher the earliest wireless messages of the war. And in that event the destination of the *Goeben* and *Breslau* might have been gauged rather more accurately in England than was the case and the campaign in the Dardanelles would have taken a very different turn.

As they have never been printed before, it may be interesting to give here translations of the two most important of them.

```
                              4 August, 1914, 1.35. a.m.
Berlin (via Nauen) to Goeben
No.51, Alliance with Turkey. Goeben and Breslau to
proceed immediately to Constantinople.
                                        Admiralty Staff


                              10 August, 1914. 2.15. p.m.
Nauen to Goeben
It is of the greatest importance to go to Constantinople
as quickly as possible in order thereby to compel Turkey
to side with us on the basis of the treaty that has been
concluded. The Ambassador has been informed direct.
Acknowledge.
                                        Admiralty Staff
```

At this time, however, there was still hope in the ID that with Fitzmaurice and others working for us, it would be possible to get a peaceful passage through the Straits. Indeed, I still believe that with the steps which we had already taken in the ID we might have been able to do so, but for the effect of an intercepted wireless from the German Emperor.

In none of the official histories or volumes of memoirs have I seen any mention of this particular affair.

Here I must say a word or two about the secret negotiations for which we had made ourselves responsible.

Sometime in December Cozens-Hardy had brought to my office a civil engineer, Mr George Griffin Eady, who, he thought, would be most useful to us. Mr Eady had held for some years a high and responsible position with Sir John Jackson Ltd, the contractors. He knew the Near East peculiarly well. At the outbreak of war he had been in Constantinople and on friendly terms with many of the most influential Turks, and it was he who on my asking for other men who could help us, had introduced me to Fitzmaurice and to Edwin Whittall, a member of one of the best-known commercial houses in Constantinople. They were able to give us a very clear idea of the general Turkish situation, and by the end of January all three of them were in the Balkans.

Their main object was simple: it was to try to persuade Turkey to break with her new Allies and to allow us a peaceful passage through the Straits. To bring about any such break there seemed to be only two alternatives: either to promote a revolution aimed against Enver Pasha and the Young Turk party which was then in power, or, what in the absence of a suitable leader seemed to be the better plan, to persuade the more reasonable members of Enver's party to make peace with ourselves.

They were soon in a position to report that of all the Young Turks, Talaat Bey, Minister of the Interior, would be the best man to approach. After an unsuccessful attempt to be allowed to enter Constantinople, Whittall succeeded in getting into touch with Talaat at Dedeagach. One of his employees was the adopted son of the Grand Rabbi, a strong Anglophile, and this man had no great difficulty in persuading the Grand Rabbi to see Talaat. Their interview was not unfavourable, but unfortunately there were heavy Russian reverses at the time, and Talaat became frightened. Further meetings, however, were held, and finally Talaat, who was now acting with the Grand Vizier, agreed to send an emissary to Dedeagach.

It then became necessary to state our terms in detail, and here there arose the expected difficulties. Unfortunately, secret pourparlers in other directions had taken place, and we had an agreement with Russia about the future of Constantinople and of the Turks in Europe. By consequence Whittall and Eady were unable to give the required undertakings. Repeatedly they cabled home begging for a reconsideration of their instructions, but this the First Lord, to whom all their cables were submitted, was unable to sanction. Our hands were tied. Nevertheless we by no means gave up hope. Powerful sections, we knew, of Turkish opinion were in favour of these negotiations. Reports, too, from Constantinople itself had shown us that many of its most influential citizens would welcome an immediate break with the Germans who had never been loved and were no longer trusted. Prayers were even being offered up in the mosques for our arrival. And in these circumstances I had judged it politic to strengthen the hands of Whittall and others.

At the beginning of March, however, it became necessary to press for a quick decision, and we therefore telegraphed to say that henceforth each day's delay must inevitably bring with it a lowering of the price which we would be prepared to pay. On 5 March for instance the price offered for the complete surrender of the Dardanelles with the removal of all mines was £500,000, with a similar sum for the *Goeben* undamaged. But three days later the price for the battleship had been reduced to £100,000. Even so there seemed reason to suppose that when the actual meeting took place at Dedeagach on the 15th, we might be able to strike a bargain, and I had, on my own responsibility, guaranteed much larger sums than those mentioned above.

Then on the 13th a telegram was brought to me from the German Emperor, and it seemed to me to be of such importance that I took it at once to the First Sea Lord's Room:

```
                                            No.2505 V
                                             12.3.15
                                   Received 12.14 P.M.

From Nauen
To Constantinople
                  MOST  SECRET
German Constantinople
For Admiral Usedom. HM Kaiser has received the report
and telegram relating to the Dardanelles. Everything
conceivable is being done here to arrange the supply
of ammunition. For political reasons it is necessary
to maintain a confident tone in Turkey. HM the Kaiser
requests you to use your influence in this direction.
The sending of a German or Austrian submarine is being
seriously considered.
                              By command of the Highest
                                          v. Muller
```

It was not difficult to imagine the contents of von Usedom's report. There must be a serious shortage of ammunition.

Lord Fisher, I was told, had gone to the First Lord's room, and there I found him standing with Mr Churchill by the fireplace.

'First Sea Lord,' said I, 'we have just received this.'

Lord Fisher took the message, read it aloud, and waved it over his head. 'By God,' he shouted, 'I'll go through tomorrow!'

Mr Churchill, equally excited, seized hold of the telegram and read it through again for his own satisfaction. 'That means,' he said, 'they've come to the end of their ammunition.'

'Tomorrow!' repeated Lord Fisher, and at that moment I believe that he was as enthusiastic as ever Mr Churchill had been about the whole Dardanelles campaign. 'We shall probably lose six ships, but I'm going through.'

The First Lord nodded. 'Then get the orders out.'

And there and then Lord Fisher sat down at Mr Churchill's table and began to draft out the necessary orders.

I was about to return to my room when Mr Churchill turned to me and asked for the latest news from Whittall and the others, and it was then that I told him of the large sum of money I had personally guaranteed.

He stared at me. 'How much?'

'Three million pounds,' I replied, 'with power to go to four million if necessary,' and as I mentioned these figures they did seem to be extraordinarily large.

He was frowning. 'Who authorised this?' he demanded.

'I did, First Lord.'

'But, the Cabinet surely knows nothing about it?'

'No, it does not. But if we were to get peace, or if we were to get a peaceful passage for that amount, I imagine they'd be glad enough to pay.'

There came one of those moments when dropped pins are supposed to be heard. Then Mr Churchill turned to Lord Fisher who was still busily writing. 'Do you hear what this man has done? He's told his people they can go up to four million to buy a peaceful passage! On his own!'

'What!' cried Lord Fisher, starting up from his chair. 'Four million? No, no. I tell you I'm going through tomorrow, or as soon as the preparations can be completed.' He turned to me. 'Cable at once to stop all negotiations. All. No. Let the offer for the *Goeben* remain. But nothing else. We're going through.'

There was nothing to be done but to obey orders. Naturally I felt considerable regret that the work already done on these intelligence lines should now be thrown away, but in view of Lord Fisher's emphatic statement and the First Lord's concurrence, I could not see how the large sum of money which was involved could ever be approved by the Cabinet, if the naval operation now being ordered were successful.

The necessary cables were sent, and although they were not received until after the Dedeagach meeting, they not only rendered any future discussions useless but also destroyed the belief in Turkish minds of our good faith.

It may seem curious that I had chosen to bear so great a responsibility myself instead of approaching the Cabinet; but as I have said before often enough, the essential point in all such transactions is that they should be known to as few people as possible. No single member of the Cabinet could have approved, and I had had no wish to commit the First Lord in any way. Yet ironically enough, within a few weeks, when the valiant attack on 18 March had proved unsuccessful, the Cabinet were asking me to spare no expense to win over the Turks. Unfortunately it was then too late.

I pass on to a painful matter which can only be properly understood if it be borne in mind that for some weeks before his resignation Lord Fisher had been a tired man. The strain under which he worked would have been terrific in any case; as it was, his position was made all the more irksome owing to the divergence between his own views and those of the First Lord. He was the one man besides Lord Kitchener in whom the public wholeheartedly believed, but he was not a member of the War Council, and he was obliged to serve under a First Lord who, though from the best of motives, was frequently usurping executive functions which were properly his. And gradually we in the Admiralty could not help becoming aware that the Fisher we had known was no longer with us. In his place was a sorely harassed and disillusioned man who was overtaxing his strength in the attempt to carry on. He might still on occasion show the old flashes of brilliance, but, beneath the surface, all was far from being well. In these critical days he could display a nervous tension which only remained hidden from those outside owing to the tireless efforts of his naval secretary. At any moment, we felt, the breaking point would come.

The story of his resignation and the political crisis which it engendered has been told many times, and I would not attempt to retell it had it not fallen to my lot to play, all unwillingly, a tiny part in the business.

On Saturday 15 May Lord Fisher did not come to the Admiralty. I saw him with George Lambert in the Mall, apparently in a state of great excitement, and wondered what was amiss. Rumours were flying about all that day, but it was only on the Sunday that we learnt definitely of his resignation. The other Sea Lords at once sent him a joint letter begging him to reconsider his decision, and on that same day Mr Churchill was able to show the Prime Minister a reconstituted board. By the Monday, however, Mr Asquith, who at that time was using every endeavour to persuade Lord Fisher to withdraw his resignation, had decided upon a reconstruction of the government and it was while Mr Churchill was with him in Downing Street that we intercepted an important message. The German fleet had chosen this moment of all others to come out.

Immediately the political issues were forgotten. We were to learn soon enough that the German fleet had emerged for no other reason than to cover the mine-laying operations on the Dogger Bank, but on that Monday afternoon we knew no more than that the German commander-in-chief intended to 'attack by day'. It might very well be that 'der Tag' had actually dawned. In the War Room there was the most feverish activity. Mr Churchill had dashed back from Downing Street, but at this moment of crisis there was no First Sea Lord in his place. At little more than a moment's notice Sir Frederick Hamilton, the Second Sea Lord, had been called in to carry out the duties of First Sea Lord. Both he and Sir Arthur Wilson, who was still holding his advisory post, slept that night at the First Lord's house adjoining the Admiralty in order to be ready for any new move. At dawn they were in the War Room again, where they remained until it became clear, about half past ten, that we need to do nothing. The German Fleet had reached its home waters again.

The next morning just before noon I received a message from the Second Sea Lord to go and see him. I had a great personal regard for Sir Frederick Hamilton. He was a fine sailor and a great gentleman, the kind of man with whom everybody was pleased to serve. I found him alone in his room, obviously upset, and was rather startled when he locked the door behind me. He pushed a chair up to his table and asked me to sit down.

'Hall,' he said in his quiet courtly way, 'I want you to do something for me. It's something …' he paused and seemed unable to go on, 'something I can't order you to do, but something I'd earnestly ask you to do.'

There came another pause, and I waited. I had not a notion what he was about to say, though I knew that he had been up to the War Room.

'I want you,' he said at last, 'to take such steps as will make it impossible for Lord Fisher ever to return to the Admiralty. I consider him to be a real danger. He is past his work, and no longer …'

'But, sir,' I interrupted, 'I understood he'd resigned.'

'The resignation has not been accepted. It may not be accepted. The public will never understand. And I believe the Prime Minister is still hoping to get him back. That mustn't be. On Sunday we asked him to return. You know what has just happened in the War Room. This is no time for personalities. If the Germans had remained out … No, Hall, it must never happen again. We have changed our minds. We are agreed …'

'But surely sir,' I broke in again, 'this is a matter for the Sea Lords?'

'No, Hall, we can't act. If we were to make representations on these lines, we should be suspected, not unreasonably, of motives of self-interest. You must see we can't act.'

I sat there, staring at him. No, the Sea Lords would not act themselves and they were asking me to do a very hard thing. I felt that they were sincere in thinking themselves right, but I could not help being uncomfortably aware that if I agreed to act for them I might very easily be ruining myself. I could not give away their confidence, no matter what steps were to be taken, and anything that I might say on the matter outside this room would have to appear to be coming from myself alone.

'Yes,' I said, 'I see you believe you can't act for yourselves, and I'll do my best, but it's a most unpleasant job you've given me.'

'I can think of none more unpleasant,' he agreed gravely, 'but I believe it's got to be done.'

I walked back to my own room in no very happy frame of mind. By this time I was becoming well accustomed to dealing with matters which could hardly be called strictly naval. I had met a great number of politicians and seen to some extent how their minds worked. I had met those who represented the great business houses and come to understand more or less their points of view. And I had worked with these men with, I think, a minimum of friction. But this was an altogether different business. It would be so easy to utter the wrong word, to suggest unwittingly that under cover of promoting the public interest I was grinding some axe of my own. The more I thought about it the less I liked the idea. Only the previous day *The Times* in its leading article had suggested that the time had come to put a seaman at the head of the Admiralty and mentioned Lord Fisher as the obvious man for the post. And I could hardly doubt that this article exactly expressed the views of the great majority of our people. However, I had promised to do what I could, and the sooner my part in the matter were over the better.

My first idea was to ask to see the Prime Minister himself. I had come to hold Mr Asquith in the greatest respect. There were those, some of them great personal friends of my own, who were openly regretting that such a man remained at the head of affairs. Admirable no doubt in peace time, they declared, but no leader for a nation at war. Yet on every occasion on which I had come into personal contact with him, he had shown to conspicuous advantage. I liked and trusted him. I admired his cool courage in the face of all manner of attack. To myself, too, he had shown the greatest kindness. But it was one thing to be summoned to Downing Street to give information on a specific point of intelligence, and quite another to proffer advice unasked, and particularly advice which, it seemed, might not prove too acceptable.

I was still wondering whether I would take the risk when a second idea suggested itself. There would be the same risk to myself, but it seemed a much sounder plan. In such a crisis as this the Prime Minister would naturally have close friends outside the Government who would be in his full confidence. If, then, I could see somebody in that position, my task might be made slightly easier. And immediately one name occurred to me: Lord Reading.

At this time he was Lord Chief Justice, and I was personally unknown to him; but on the previous day I had appeared as a witness in his court at the trial of Kuepferle, the spy who was to hang himself in his cell the next morning, and I had been extraordinarily impressed not only by his high qualities as a judge but also by the general charm of his manner. Moreover, I knew from several sources to what a great extent the Prime Minister relied at this time on his advice. He was obviously the man, and when I took Dick Herschell into my confidence, he at once agreed with me and suggested his own flat as a meeting place.

I lost no time. A few minutes after twelve o'clock I was speaking to the Lord Chief Justice on the telephone, asking him whether he could make it convenient to see me that afternoon at Lord Herschell's flat on a matter of urgent public importance. Luckily Kuepferle's trial had been adjourned until the Thursday, and he was free. He at once agreed to come, and I spent the next two hours preparing my case. Whatever I said, I knew that I must be ready for cross-examination and nobody was willing to face Rufus Isaacs unless he was sure of his ground. Yet on consideration the ground did seem to be secure, and as I walked with Herschell across to his flat, I knew more or less what I would say.

At 3.30 Lord Reading was shown in, and I at once placed all my cards on the table. I told him that I knew I was putting my whole future in his hands, but hoped to make him understand that I was acting solely in the public interest. I then explained as well as I could the growing difficulty at the Admiralty of getting organised work done. I mentioned the conditions under which a man like Crease was working, and the repeated friction between Lord Fisher and Mr Churchill. I said bluntly that in my opinion Lord Fisher was in no fit state to continue at his post, and exhorted our visitor to represent to the Prime Minister the importance of accepting the preferred resignation without delay.

I must have spoken about ten minutes, and Lord Reading listened without interruption. But when I had finished he cross-examined me for nearly half an hour, and afterwards Dick Herschell told me that he had never heard anything like it. 'Rufus Isaacs at his very best,' said he, 'and I'm glad that my part was only that of host.' Questions, indeed, followed question, some purely technical but others so fashioned as to make sure of my motive. I cannot pretend to recall more than their gist, but I do remember the last two or three of them.

'Do you yourself object to serving under Lord Fisher?' he asked.

'I'd serve under the devil,' I told him, 'if he were proficient.'

'And that would have been your answer if I had mentioned Mr Churchill instead?'

'It would.'

'Then,' said Lord Isaacs slowly, 'if either of them is to leave the Admiralty, which would you suggest it be?'

It was the crucial question for which I had been waiting. 'Regretfully,' I told him, 'I have to say, both!'

'And why?'

'Because if you wish, as you must, to maintain any confidence between the Fleet and the Board of Admiralty, you can't keep a First Lord who will appear to have driven out of office a man like Lord Fisher. The navy would never forgive him.'

Lord Reading nodded, and for a moment or two there was silence. 'You are quite right,' he said at last, 'when you say that you have put your whole future in my hands, and if you had answered my questions differently I would have broken you. But I am now satisfied that your view of what is required is correct, and I will see the Prime Minister at once. I shall not mention your name unless he asks for it. Good-bye.'

Two days later it was announced that Mr Balfour had been appointed First Lord, and the following morning Lord Fisher's resignation was accepted.

He never returned to the Admiralty. More than once efforts were made to get him back, but they did not succeed. When Sir John Jellicoe had taken up his duties as First Sea Lord, it was seriously suggested to him that Lord Fisher should work under him as controller to the navy and third sea lord, but nothing came of the proposal. And he himself made one very curious attempt to return after more than two years' work as President of the Board of Inventions and Research. I do not use the word 'curious' because of his making the endeavour: so much was to be expected of a man who so thoroughly believed in himself and could write to a friend that after his departure 'we had two years of ineffable apathy at the Admiralty'. I use the word because on this occasion he chose to approach the authorities through myself, although only a month before he had been threatening to resign from the Board of Inventions on my account.

This Board had been set up in July 1915. Men of the greatest distinction like Sir J.J. Thomson and Sir Charles Parsons served with Lord Fisher upon it, and it did some most admirable work. At the same time it seemed to me to be at times responsible for unnecessarily bitter criticism of Admiralty methods of combating the submarine menace, and I do not think that I was altogether wrong in attributing most of this criticism to Lord Fisher.

In his eyes we were the 'permanent Expert limpets' who were for ever obstructing their work, and I am afraid that I myself occupied the unenviable position of being considered to be the least competent and most objectionable of them all. It is only fair to add that one of the board's information duties was to assist in designing material for our anti-submarine campaign, and in order to help them in this work, it had been arranged that the Admiralty should report to the board all successful actions against submarines. On 16 July 1917, however, the further request was made that a report of every action with submarines, successful or not, should be sent to them.

In due course this request came down to the ID, and on looking through the docket of papers it seemed to me that there was some hesitation on the part of those in positions of higher authority than my own in making a suitable answer. To me there could be only one reply, and I made it.

```
                                                    28.7.17
ID Minute.
I do not recommend approval of this proposal. The BIR¹ can
carry out research on lines suggested by the Admiralty.
The extension of circulation of these reports is to be
deprecated. It will only lead to irresponsible criticism.
                                                    W R H
```

Now the usual custom at the Admiralty, and, indeed, in most government offices, in dealing with any such Minute, was to extract its general sense and draft a suitably diplomatic letter from it. In this case for some reason or other this was not done. Unluckily for me, the original docket with my Minute attached was sent to the Board of Inventions.

I was unaware of what had been done until some days later a violent ring called me to the First Lord.

It did not need more than a glance to see that something was wrong. Sir Eric Geddes was champing in his room like a wild horse.

Waving a piece of paper in his hand, he cried out: 'What the devil have you been doing?'

Purposely I began to give him a literal reply. 'Lately we have been exceedingly busy with a new chart-system ...'

'No, no, no. I mean, what have you been doing to Lord Fisher?'

So that was the trouble! 'Nothing,' I said. 'He's not at the Admiralty. I've done nothing at all to Lord Fisher.'

'Haven't you! Then read that.'

He thrust the paper, dated 2 August 1917, into my hands.

```
The Remarks of Admiral W.R. Hall are such that it seems
to me that unless he is removed it will be necessary for
me to resign.
                                                    Fisher
```

---

1   BIR – the Admiralty's Board of Invention and Research.

I had to do some quick thinking. Sir Eric Geddes had been at the Admiralty but a very few months. He had been First Lord for little more than a fortnight. But already he had made his mark and given us some insight into his character. Like Lord Fisher he was a man with great driving power who believed in himself. I took a plunge. 'Then it doesn't seem to matter much, First Lord,' I said, 'what I've been doing.'

He stared. 'What d'you mean?'

'I mean,' said I very solemnly, 'you've got your orders to dismiss me.'

'Orders!' His tones were rising. 'I don't take orders from Fisher.'

'Then, Sir, if that be the case, you'd better tell him so,' and I shot out of the room.

But I was obliged to eat humble pie. Neither the First Lord nor myself wanted a row, and my second minute was rather more politely expressed:

```
First Lord
I regret to find that the BIR have read the word
'irresponsible' in my minute in the wrong sense.
The meaning that I intended to convey was that I
deprecated the circulation of reports to those who are
not responsible for the operations.
```

And there the little matter ended. Yet barely a month had passed before Lord Fisher was seeking my assistance to engineer his return to the Admiralty.

Early in the morning of 4 October the telephone rang in Claude Serocold's room. He came in to tell me that the editor of the *Daily Mail* wanted to see me at once on a matter of some urgency. Unfortunately Tom Marlowe was confined to his house with a bad cold: could I go round? It happened that I was unusually busy at the time. 'You go,' I suggested to Serocold, 'and act for me.'

At lunchtime I was given details of their interview. Lord Fisher, it seemed, had had a conversation with Mr H.W. Wilson of the *Daily*

Mail staff, in the course of which he had asked that a message might be conveyed through Tom Marlowe to me.

The gist of this message was that I should be asked to work in the closest cooperation with Lord Fisher with the object of securing his return to the Admiralty. Only in this way could the country be saved. Mr Wilson had seen his editor, but Tom Marlowe, with whom by this time I had come to be on the most intimate terms, felt that it would be wholly useless to hand on any such message. He greatly doubted whether I would regard it as bona fide, and even if I wished to consider the proposition he did not see how he could play any useful part in the matter. However, as Lord Fisher had insisted on his seeking my opinion, he had done so.

'But, surely,' I said to Serocold, 'there was only one answer to give?'

'Oh yes,' he replied with a smile, 'and I gave it.'

Yet I am convinced that Lord Fisher was not acting from any selfish motive. He was now a very tired old man, and his judgment was not what it had been; but he still believed in himself, and he knew that throughout the country there were thousands who still regretted his retirement. I believe that it was only a warped sense of duty which suggested to him so curious a move. Unfortunately the time had gone by when it could be seriously entertained.

By a coincidence it was on this same day that Sir Frederick Hamilton died.

THE ZIMMERMANN TELEGRAM AND AMERICA'S ENTRY INTO THE WAR

I need to note at the start that initials only were used in the Mexican affair. Also at one point 'T' and the British Minister are made to appear as two people. The name of the English printer is not given, and the man who was really his brother is here called his 'best friend'. All intercepts here printed have already been published, most of them by Lansing in America during the war, otherwise in Page's Letters.

If further evidence were needed to show the importance in intelligence work of ignoring no item of information, however trivial it may seem to be, it is to be found in the curious chain of events which, beginning in the summer of 1916, led in the early part of the next year to the exposure of what is now generally known as the Zimmermann Telegram. Again and again in the ID we found that the biggest developments could be traced back to the unlikeliest sources, and so it was here. At one end of the panorama you have a slightly ridiculous request for a decoration; at the other you see the United States enter the war.

Moreover I know of no other incident in my experience as an intelligence officer which better illustrates at once the difficulties of using to the best advantage such information as is obtained and the great and sometimes grave risks which have to be taken to bring about the desired end. Our exposure of the Zimmermann Telegram was in the nature of a huge gamble. Luckily it came off. The steps which we took did in point of fact turn out to be about the best that we could have taken; what is equally important; they were taken at the right moment. But very easily indeed this gamble might not have come off, and in that case I do not care to think of what might have happened.

The true story of the telegram has never been fully told. The main facts relating to the actual exposure are accurately set forth in Dr Page's Letters, but the several steps which made this possible are now detailed for the first time, and if I give them in considerable detail it is mainly because so many inaccurate accounts have strayed into print.

It may be best to begin by summarising very briefly the general position of affairs, so far as the ID was concerned, towards the end of 1916.

It was a most anxious time, and from my point of view a peculiar time, for to the study of enemy movements which was our primary duty was added the necessity for an intensive study of American politics. The one question of paramount importance was this: at what date would the Germans open their campaign of unrestricted submarine warfare? That it must come sooner or later we were fairly certain. 'You will have seen by Lloyd George's speech,' I had written to Gaunt at the end of September, 'that for once in our lives we hold the same views. It has been a struggle to get the ministers out in the open and say exactly what the people of England think, and not what the politicians would like them to think. The Germans, I think, will start their submarine warfare within the next few weeks. They have tried for their armistice with neutrals and failed. I think they are now trying to secure an armistice direct and will fail again, and when convinced that we mean war, they will go all out.' After their abortive attempt to make peace, indeed, we could hardly doubt that there would be any long delay. For some time, too, we had been aware that they had been endeavouring in various ways to gauge the effect on our mercantile marine if the submarines were permitted to attack at sight all vessels found in the war zone. We knew, of course, the reason why their submarine attacks had almost stopped earlier in the year. It was not, as they alleged, in deference to American opinion, but because their existing submarines were being refitted and new crews trained. But by October they had about 200 submarines ready, some of which had crossed the Atlantic and were operating very close to American waters, the 'long-distance blockade'. On 7 October, *U.53* had appeared at Newport, Rhode Island, and during the next two days had sunk no less than nine merchant vessels off the Nantucket lightship and in circumstances which led us to hope that American patience might be nearing its end. Within a few weeks' time the *Deutschland* had arrived for the third time at New York, carrying with her £2,000,000 in securities and, incidentally, a new codebook, and President Wilson had been re-elected. We knew that he would never declare war unless he was convinced that all the States, and not only those in the East, desired it. At the moment, indeed, he was endeavouring to promote a peace which the Allies had warned him they could not accept, but we hoped for the best. Meanwhile more Notes were passing, and as usual the Germans had promised to conform strictly to the dictates of international law.

At home the position was exceedingly difficult. There was not only a shortage of men, but a shortage of food as well. There were distinct signs of war-weariness, and criticism was being directed against most government departments. In particular the Admiralty was singled out for the fiercest attacks. Complaints were made, and not only in the press, that the board had become stale. There were angry meetings in the city and demands for a more forthright policy to deal with the submarine menace. At the end of November Sir John Jellicoe replaced Sir Henry Jackson as First Sea Lord. Less than a week later Mr Asquith had resigned, and in Mr Lloyd George's Cabinet Sir Edward Carson had become First Lord, with his predecessor, Mr Balfour, at the Foreign Office.

But by the end of December we could not say at what precise date unrestricted submarine warfare would begin, and there was nothing to do but wait and prepare.

Now it happened that for some time one of our best decypherers had been at work on one of the German diplomatic codes. It was the one which was usually known as 13040. And here, perhaps, is the best place to introduce the man who was chiefly responsible for its reconstruction. Nigel de Grey had come from the RNAS to Sir Alfred Ewing's department in June 1915. Before the war his work as a publisher had not led him to pay any attention to cryptography, but once in 40 OB he had almost immediately shown a remarkable flair for the work, and so soon as the size of staff permitted, he had, with one or two others, been taken off the usual watches and given all his time to research work. There had been a pile of undecyphered stuff to work upon, but nothing else. Yet by this time de Grey was rapidly reaching the stage when he could understand at any rate the general sense of nearly all dispatches sent in the 13040 code.

So far as we then knew, this code was used only in letters to and from Germany. Such letters were usually sent in duplicate to at least two accommodation addresses, and one day one of them came into de Grey's hands. It was not in itself a communication of any great interest, yet for us it was of the greatest possible importance, showing us, as it did, that in certain quarters diplomatic privileges were being seriously misused, and affording further reason, if it were wanted, why our examination of mails on all neutral ships should continue to be as close as we could make it. It was a letter, written on a double sheet of blue foolscap, from the German Minister in Mexico to von Bethmann Hollweg, and it ran, in translation, as follows:

```
                                        8th March 1916
ECKARDT TO VON BETHMANN HOLLWEG
The Swedish Charge d'Affaires here, Herr F. Cronholm
has, since he has been here, made no concealment of
his sympathy for Germany and placed himself in close
connection with this Legation. Since the closing of the
Brazilian and Guatemalan Legations in August last year
he is the only neutral diplomat through whom information
```

```
from the enemy camp can be obtained. Further, he arranges
the conditions for the official telegraphic traffic with
your Excellency. In this connection he is obliged every
time, often late at night, personally to go to the
telegraph office to hand in the dispatches. Herr Cronholm
has not got a Swedish order but a Chilean one. I beg to
submit to your Excellency, if your Excellency approves,
that Herr Cronholm should be recommended in the proper
quarter for the Kronenorden of the 2nd class.
   In order to raise no suspicion on the side of our
opponents, it would be more advisable to treat the decoration
if it be granted, as a secret matter till the end of the war,
and only to inform the recipient and his Government of it,
and then only under the seal of promise not to publish his
investiture until after the end of the war.
```

De Grey brought me this letter, and although neither of us had the slightest idea to what Herr Cronholm's desire for a decoration would lead us, it was clear that steps would have to be taken to have all the Swedish Foreign Office cypher telegrams brought to us for examination. Arrangements were soon made for this to be done, and in many cases it was found that after a few Swedish groups our old friend 13040 would appear. Our excitement, moreover, may be imagined when through this means we discovered the route by which Bernstorff was communicating with his government!

It was a question which had been worrying us for some time.[1] How did he get his telegrams to Berlin? 'We have traced nearly every route,' I had written to Gaunt at the beginning of May, 'and I am really reduced to the following: he sends them down to Buenos Aires, thence across to Valparaiso. From there I cannot make out where they are sent, whether

---

1   See maps 5a and 5b.

via China or Russia through the connivance of a neutral legation or not.'
Now we knew which Legation was being responsible, and as a result of
that knowledge we were in a short time reading all the essential parts
of Bernstorff's dispatches and the replies of his government. In this way
we found ourselves in full possession, for all practical purposes, of the
enemy's every move in the diplomatic game of the moment, and knew
from the Ambassador's admirably clear dispatches the points of greatest
importance in Mr Wilson's fluctuating policy. In addition it afforded us
an insight into some of the devious ways of German agents all over the
American continent.

As yet, however, we had no means of intercepting such German or
Swedish messages as passed only over American soil. There might be
little information of value in them which we should not receive when
they were forwarded on from Buenos Aires, but it would be well to have
a second string to our bow, and I therefore asked 'H', a good friend of
mine then in Mexico City, if he could do anything in the matter.

'H', as it happened, already had his suspicions about Herr Cronholm's
activities, and he had given the gist of them to another branch of our
intelligence service. In his letters home, moreover, he had included
detailed pictures of the various Legations in Mexico City. They made
up an odd little world by themselves, those Legations, and the German
with von Eckardt at its head remained the oddest of them all. Von Papen
himself had been there before the war, and had not scrupled to tell our
own Minister that he had been ordered to study Mexican methods
of blowing up trains. There had been, too, a cheery fellow called von
Hintze, who at this time was giving us some trouble in Hong Kong.
And there was still a grossly fat, good-natured secretary called Magnus
who, according to 'H', had continued to pester the British Minister with
invitations to dinner after war had been declared, and thought it churlish
of him to refuse. Poor simple Magnus! He was stabbed in the stomach
one day outside his own Legation, and his fat saved him; but it did not
save him from some most anxious hours later on.

And then there was Cronholm himself, a coarse, vulgar, noisy brute, just the kind of man who would want to collect decorations. Obviously he was on very good terms with his German colleagues, but was he actually working for them? 'H' had gone to work very skilfully, and by finding out from various sources the size of his telegraph bills and what allowances he was receiving on that account from his own government, had formed his own conclusions.

Now we were able to give him proof that his conclusions were right, and he in his turn was able to be of the greatest assistance to us, for in a rather odd way he was enabled to secure for us German cypher messages which passed between Washington and Mexico City.

It will be remembered that during the war there had been repeated revolutions in Mexico, and they were not even now at an end. In a short while United States troops under General Pershing were to cross the borders on their ill-fated Villa expedition. The point of importance to us lay in the fact that as each new conqueror took charge of the capital city one of the first things he did was to declare the currency of his predecessor valueless and issue some of his own. This was a matter of no great difficulty. All that was necessary was to print something new on small bits of cardboard – they resembled railway-tickets and were known as *cartonés* (boards) – and call them money. They were, most of them, worth no more than a penny or two, but there were numerous forgeries always in circulation, and the matter became so serious that President Carranza had given orders that any such forgery should be punishable by death.

It was shortly after this order had been made that a printer, an Englishman, happened to return to his workshop unexpectedly one Saturday afternoon. Naturally his workmen, all of them Mexicans, had gone. To his astonishment and dismay he found on a table a neat pile of these *cartonés* and the plates from which they had been printed. In his excitement he made the worst possible mistake: he locked up the forgeries and the plates in the safe. Then he rushed out to consult his best friend as to what he had better do. Meanwhile the workman who been responsible for the forgeries returned to get his money, and, realising what must have happened, sought to save his own skin by getting in first with a denunciation. This he was able to do, with the result that the unfortunate printer was arrested the same afternoon, ordered to open his safe, where of course the *cartonés* and the plates were found, hurried off to a drumhead court martial and condemned to be shot at dawn on the Monday.

Luckily the printer was not without other friends, among them 'H', at whose request the British minister interested himself in the case. There were hurried consultations, and the minister made himself responsible for the so-called criminal. He did more. He argued that if an Englishman intended to commit forgery he would aim rather higher than penny or twopenny notes. He persuaded the authorities to examine the case rather more closely, and so obtained the printer's release.

It was an unpleasant affair while it lasted, but it had good results for us, for both the printer and his friend in thanking 'H' for his good offices declared that if at any time there was anything they could do to show their gratitude they would do it, no matter what it might be.

I have only to add that the friend at this time was working in the telegraph office.

And it was this arrangement, a mere precaution in the first instance, which was not only to have an important effect later on in establishing the genuineness of the Zimmermann Telegram but was also to play its part in covering our tracks.

For some time these Mexican messages were not strikingly helpful, but they were not without interest. 'The Swedish representative', Eckardt was telegraphing on 1 September, 'fears English suspicion and complaints in Stockholm on account of his frequent telegrams.' Wherefore he suggested that for the future his 'reports about ships' might be allowed to lapse. And we were not altogether surprised to learn the next month that the German Minister had received no reply to his letter of 8 March with regard to Cronholm's decoration. Incidentally this dispatch informed us that, 'Carranza who is now openly friendly to Germany is willing to support if necessary German submarines in Mexican waters to the best of his ability,' a piece of news which seems to be reflected in the more important dispatch sent on 12 November by Bernstorff to Eckardt:

```
WASHINGTON TO MEXICO
The Imperial Government proposes to employ the most
efficacious means to annihilate its principal enemy, and
since it designs to carry its operations to America with
the object of destroying its enemy's commerce, it will be
very valuable to have certain bases to assist the work of
its submarines both in South America and in Mexico, as,
for example, in the State of Tamaulipas. Accordingly the
Imperial Government would see with the greatest pleasure
the Mexican Government's consent to cede the necessary
permission for the establishment of a base in its
territory, on the understanding that any arrangements
completed will not involve the slightest damage to the
dignity or integrity of Mexico, since that country
will be treated like the free and independent nation
which it is. The Imperial Government, being perfectly
acquainted with the special circumstances through which
Mexico is passing at the present time, in that period of
reconstruction in which being a young country she finds
herself, would like to know what advantages Mexico would
find suitable on her part, especially in the financial and
economic crisis through which she is passing, if she
agrees to the desires of the Imperial Government.
```

Then, early in the New Year came the Zimmermann Telegram, and if our first knowledge of this surprising communication was derived from European sources, our friends in Mexico City were soon playing an important part in the complicated business that followed.

I am not likely to forget that Wednesday morning, 17 January 1917. There was the usual docket of papers to be gone through on my arrival at the office, and Claude Serocold and I were still at work when at about half-past ten de Grey came in. He seemed excited.

'DID', he began, 'do you want to bring America into the war?'

'Yes, my boy,' I answered. 'Why?'

'I've got something here which, well it's a rather astonishing message which might do the trick if we could use it. It isn't very clear, I'm afraid, but I'm sure I've got most of the important points right. It's from the German Foreign Office to Bernstorff.'

I give the telegram in the form that I first read it:

```
BERLIN TO WASHINGTON
                                               W.158
                                      16 January, 1917
Most secret for your Excellency's personal information
and to be handed on to the Imperial Minister in (?)
Mexico with ... by a safe route.
  We propose to begin on the 1 February unrestricted
submarine warfare. In doing so however we shall endeavour
to keep America neutral ...(?) If we should not (succeed
in doing so) we propose to Mexico an alliance upon the
following basis:
          (joint) conduct of war
          (joint) conclusion of peace
...
Your excellency should for the present inform the President
secretly (that we expect) war with the USA (possibly) (...
Japan) and at the same to negotiate between us and Japan
... Indecypherable sentence meaning, 'Please tell the
President that ... our submarines ... will compel England
to peace within a few months'. Acknowledge receipt.
                                             ZIMMERMANN
```

So not only had the great decision been taken, but the Germans were preparing to bring Mexico into the business!

SMS *Blücher* sinking at Jutland. (Associated Press Ltd)

Prince Henry of Prussia. (Library of Congress)

Above: *U-28* sunk in 1917.
(northatlanticblog.wordpress.com)

Right: HMS *Cornwall*.

Below: Mr Hendrikus Colijn, 1905.

Wassmuss in Persian dress.

Admiral von Tirpitz.
(Bericheid, Berlin)

John Buchan, 1915.

Count Bernstorff and friends in Washington DC. (*The Sketch*, 25 October 1916)

Above: HMS *Bristol*, 1910.

Left: SMS *Möwe*, seen from the captured liner *Appam*, 1916. (www.smsmoewe.com)

Left: Von Rintelen, the 'Dark Invader'.

Below: Black Tom explosion, Jersey City, 1916.

Above: BNI agents, Colonel Thoroton and Juan March, with Sultan Moulay Joussef, Morocco. (Thoroton Family Archive)

Right: BNI agents, Colonel Thoroton and Henryano Kerchaer, his Spanish number two, Gibraltar. (Thoroton Family Archive)

Above: Talaat Pasha. (Library of Congress)

Left: Zinoviev speaks.

SMS *Magdeburg*. (Bundesarchiv, Bild 146-2007-0221)

HMS *Russell*. (Bain News Service)

Lord Herschell, 1919. (*Room 40*, Patrick Beesly)

Reginald McKenna by Leslie Ward (spy) cartoon. (*Vanity Fair*)

Sir George Cockerill. (Walter Stoneman)

HMS *Queen Mary* explodes, Jutland, 1916. (Mondiale)

Prime Minister Herbert Henry Asquith. (Bain News Service)

Lord Kitchener, the famous poster.

Anthony Drexel's steam yacht *Sayonara*. (Patrick Langrishe, by permission of Michael W. Pocock)

On the left the 'skipper' Lieutenant Simon RNR; on the right the 'owner' Colonel McBride (actually Major Wilfred Howell). (T. Stubbs)

Karl Boy-ed, German naval attaché, Washington DC. (Library of Congress)

Franz von Papen, German military attaché, Washington DC. (Library of Congress)

HMS *Cornwallis*.

Sir Eustace d'Eyncourt.
(Library of Congress)

Russian battleship *Petropavlovsk*.

HMS *Lion*, Beatty's flagship, 'a splendid cat'.

Clara Zetkin and Rosa Luxemburg, 1910.

Emmeline Pankhurst, 1913.
(NY Bookpress, 1970)

Miss Jane Addams, 1914.
(Library of Congress)

SMS *Kronprinz Wilhelm.*

Admiral David Beatty. (*The Battle of Jutland*, John Buchan)

Left: Admiral Jellicoe as First Sea Lord. (Bain News Service)

Below: Rufus Isaacs, Lord Reading. (Bain News Service)

Above: Von Usedom (in Turkish uniform), Kaiser Wilhelm II, Enver Pasha and Vice Admiral Merten, Gallipoli, 1917.

Sir Edward Grey. (Bassano)

SMS *Goeben* renamed *Yavuz* in Sevastopol, 1918. (Europeana 1914–1918)

SMS *Breslau* renamed *Midilli*.

William Cozens-Hardy. (*Illustrated London News*)

Sir Frederick Hamilton, Second Sea Lord, 1916. (Francis Dodd)

Sir Arthur Wilson. (*The Navy & Army Illustrated*, 1898)

Arthur James Balfour.

Sir J.J. Thomson. (*The Great War*, H.W. Wilson & J.A. Hammerton)

Sir Charles Parsons.

Admiral 'Jacky' Fisher.
(Bain News Service)

Gertrude Bell in
Iraq, 1909.

Arthur Zimmermann.

Robert Lansing, US
Secretary of State. (Harris
& Ewing)

Dr Walter Hines Page. (Bain News Service)

The German freight submarine *Deutschland*, renamed *U-155*. (*Journal of the United States Artillery*)

Nigel de Grey RNAS.
(*Room 40*, Patrick Beesly)

Von Bethmann-Hollweg,
1913. (Ernst Sandau)

Paul von Hintze.
(Agence Rol)

Sir Archer Gaunt.
(*Lusitania*, Colin
Simpson)

Porfirio Díaz, President
of Mexico. (Aurelio
Escobar Castellanos
Archive)

Sir Cecil Spring
Rice.

Above: Scandinavian America Line's
SS *Frederik VIII*.

Left: Maximilian von Ratibor, German
Ambassador to Spain 1910–18. (Mundo Gráfico)

Below: Major Arnold Kalle, German military
attaché, at the Madrid embassy, 1910.
(Mundo Gráfico)

I must have read through that imperfectly decoded message three or four times without speaking a word. I gave it to Claud, and he, too, read it in silence.

'A cablegram,' I said at last, 'sent, I suppose, through Stockholm? And will it go to Buenos Aires, and thence up to Washington?'

De Grey nodded.

'And they'll probably use other routes as well.' Indeed, at least two other routes were used.[2]

'Almost certainly they will.'

I do not remember a time when I was more excited. Yet, as de Grey had pointed out, the telegram was only of importance if we could make use of it. Could we? There would have to be some very hard thinking. At the moment nothing must be done except to take all possible precautions to keep the news to our three selves.

I thanked de Grey, and asked him to bring me the original telegram in cypher.

'This,' I told him, 'is a case where standing orders must be suspended. All copies of this message, both those in cypher and your own transcripts, are to be brought straight to me. Nothing is to be put on the files. This may be a very big thing, possibly the biggest thing of the war. For the present not a soul outside this room is to be told anything at all.'

A little later the original message and its decypher were locked away in my desk and I sat down by myself to evolve a plan of campaign.

What was the position? Within a fortnight's time the fact that Germany was proposing to declare immediate unrestricted submarine warfare would be communicated by Bernstorff to the United States government. Would it be sufficient to convince President Wilson that the Germans would stick at nothing? His most recent Note had shown us something of the way in which his mind was working. It seemed that he drew little

---

2   See maps 5a and 5b.

distinction between the behaviour of the Allies and that of the Germans, or, indeed, between the justice of our cause and theirs. Were this new declaration to be sufficient, well and good, we need run no risks and the Zimmermann Telegram need never be used at all. But it was necessary to be prepared for every contingency. The new submarine warfare might not be by itself sufficient to convince the President, and in that case this new information must be made use of if we could safeguard ourselves.

But could we? I must have put the question to myself a dozen times, and each time the reply seemed to be more strongly in the negative. Publication of this particular telegram would almost certainly rouse the whole of the United States and might well force the President to declare war, but it would be at the cost of hazarding the most vital part of our intelligence system. It was imperative that we ran no risk of the Germans learning the secret of 40 OB.

Therefore the intercept already in our hands must in no circumstances be exposed.

And that, I think, must be my reply to those who may wonder why I personally needed to play any prominent part at all in the Zimmermann exposure. A cypher cablegram had been intercepted; it contained proposals for an alliance between Germany and Mexico in the event of the United States coming into the war, and beyond the fact that it gave us the date on which the Germans were intending to begin their unrestricted submarine warfare, there was nothing in it of naval interest. What, then, was there to prevent me from immediately handing it over to the Foreign Office authorities? A naval officer is not trained for foreign politics, and surely there were those who were far better able to deal with the matter than myself. Yet so far, it would seem, from taking the obvious course, I deliberately withheld all information from those best entitled to receive it until a dangerously late date, and assumed a responsibility which ought never to have been mine. Well, that may be so, but I was not altogether a free agent. This cablegram could never be used. Why then run the smallest risk of its contents becoming known to somebody who, not being familiar with every branch of our activity, might all unwittingly compromise some part or all of the work in Room 40?

No, for the present the secret must be shared by nobody except de Grey, Serocold and myself.

Yet some plan would have to be evolved, and it was while I was mentally following the route that the Zimmermann message would take, that I remembered the Bernstorff-Eckardt messages which 'H' had secured for us. But this new one, when forwarded on as it must be, from Washington to Mexico, would be only another in that series. We could probably secure a copy of it, and could anything be done with that? Not, I saw, before a break in diplomatic relations, for it was vital to keep secret the fact that 13040 was compromised so long as Bernstorff remained in Washington. But in any case we would not want to make use of it before then, and on the outbreak of unrestricted submarine warfare, even if President Wilson did not declare war, he was almost bound, in view of his warning after the *Sussex* outrage, to give the German Ambassador his passports. Then might it not be possible to use the Washington–Mexico dispatch in some way, which should make it appear as though we ourselves had nothing to do with the business? Here, I felt, the solution of the problem would lie, though as yet there was no very clear plan in my head.

There was also, of course, another question to be considered. Granted that some safe plan were to suggest itself, how were we to convince President Wilson and the American people that the Zimmermann Telegram was not a British-made hoax? Even if somebody he implicitly trusted like Mr Balfour were to give his personal assurance that the telegram was genuine, the President might not unreasonably demand the most definite proof that the message really bore the meaning which we ascribed to it, and how could that be done without giving to the Americans information of the most secret nature?

It was decidedly a difficult problem, and I must confess that many days were to pass before I saw my way clearly through the wood. Luckily there was no need for an immediate decision. No matter what happened, we could not usefully take any active steps until after the declaration of 1 February. On the other hand it was essential to keep the closest possible watch on Bernstorff and the American situation, in order to be ready at any given moment with alternative plans.

Later that day I sent for de Grey again, verified the exact route which the cablegram would follow, explained something of what was in my mind, using his knowledge of the Bernstorff dispatches to check my own estimate of the situation, and begged him to concentrate on getting the rest of the cablegram out.

And, as so often before, we watched and waited.

The German Ambassador, we knew, would be greatly upset, for all the time he had been warning Germany that unrestricted submarine warfare would inevitably bring the United States into the war. It was quite possible, indeed, that before sending on the message he would cable a final protest to Berlin. He might even be able to induce the German government to change its plans. In point of fact he made the most strenuous efforts to prevent a break. He received the Zimmermann Telegram on 19 January and it is interesting to note that the delays in transatlantic cable traffic permitted us to learn its contents before Bernstorff knew them himself. That same day he strongly urged his government to postpone the new submarine warfare for an appreciable period, a month was suggested, after their intentions had been publicly declared. Three days later the President's 'Peace without Conquest' speech to the Senate raised his hopes, though to us it was a serious blow. Then on the 28th de Grey brought me part of Bernstorff's second protest, dispatched the previous day, in which he made it quite clear that only by a postponement of the declaration could the diplomatic position be improved, and begging for a reply by wireless 'as cables always take several days'.

Here, by the way, occurred one of those incidents which make one want to tear one's hair out with vexation. A preliminary telegram to the German Foreign Office had warned us that an important interview with the President had taken place, and as soon de Grey had shown me the opening sentences I rushed back with him to Room 40 to urge on the work of translation, though I knew that the work could not be completed for some hours. Two of the officers were already at work on it and promised that their task should be finished with all possible speed. My anxiety, indeed, to know the President's attitude was acute. There was, I well remember, an atmosphere of excitement in the room, and the cheerful feeling that great things were doing. But, happening to pass through the room a short while later I was met with long dismal faces. The early and later parts of the dispatch were in 13040, but the vital sentences which reported President Wilson's own words were in a new code about which we knew nothing at all! It was clear at any rate what one part of the *Deutschland's* cargo had been. However, enough of the dispatch was decyphered to give us the general tenor of the interview, as also of the Chancellor's reply two days later to Bernstorff. We knew that it was couched in the negative, and the die was cast.

Then on successive days Bernstorff presented the declaration, the new submarine warfare began, and President Wilson broke off diplomatic relations with Germany. As it happened, it fell to my lot to be the first to give the American embassy the news. At nine o'clock on that Saturday evening I hurried round to Grosvenor Place with a message from Gaunt. 'Bernstorff has just been given his passports. I shall probably get drunk tonight.'

To our dismay, however, although not altogether to our surprise, matters went no further. Cables from Washington and New York were warning us to be prepared for delays and even for nothing more than the state of 'armed neutrality' which Mr Wilson was about to proclaim. It became necessary to take action, and on 5 February I saw Lord Hardinge at the Foreign Office, and showed him the amplified decode which de Grey was now able to produce.

By this time my plans had matured sufficiently to allow me to put forward several suggestions. In the first place it would be necessary to obtain a copy of the Bernstorff–Eckardt dispatch. 'H', as it happened, was no longer in Mexico City, but his place had been taken by 'T', who was fully aware of what was afoot in the telegraph office. I did not anticipate much trouble there, and with this message in our hands we would be on fairly safe ground. For even though it became necessary to give secret information to the American government, we would be dealing with a dispatch which had never been near Europe, and I had now, I hoped, derived a means whereby only Americans would be concerned in the business at all. For this purpose, however, I wanted Mr Balfour's assistance, whether in his official capacity as Foreign Secretary or privately as the impeccable elder statesman, I did not mind, and so of course it became necessary to see Lord Hardinge.

As I had expected, the Permanent Secretary remained his useful cool self, interested but cautious. He asked for my views and promised to lay them before Mr Balfour. No immediate decision, he thought, could be taken, but for this I had been prepared. On the other hand there was no reason why steps should not now be taken to obtain the additional evidence which we should require in the event of an exposure, and on the following day 'T' was asked to secure copies of all telegrams sent by Bernstorff to Eckardt since 18 January. These were to be sent on to Gaunt, who was to forward them on to me as he received them, but put into our own cypher.

And once again we were obliged to wait.

There came a second telegram from Zimmermann, sent direct to Mexico, and for the sake of completion I give it here:

Berlin
8th Feb. 1917

Most Secret. Decypher personally.
Provided there is no danger of secret being betrayed to USA you are desired without further delay to broach the question of an Alliance to the President. The definite

conclusion of an Alliance, however, is dependent on the
outbreak of war between Germany and USA. The President
might even now, on his own account, sound Japan.

If the President declines from fear of subsequent
revenge you are empowered to offer him a definitive
alliance after conclusion of peace provided Mexico
succeeds in drawing Japan into the alliance.

ZIMMERMANN

There was, however, considerable danger of the secret being betrayed
to the United States, for two days later we learnt that 'T' had secured
the three or four cables which we wanted. He took infinite pains to
recypher their contents into one of our own cyphers, so that neither
Germans nor Mexicans should suspect what was being done, and what
our decypherers in New York thought about the extra labour which this
involved was expressed in good strong language. But they worked like
Trojans, with the result that on 19 February we received in London a
cabled copy of the Bernstorff–Eckardt message of 19 January.

By this time de Grey had made such considerable advance with his
reconstruction of 13040 that he was able to provide us with what was
practically a perfect transcript, and I give it here in the form in which it
was finally published, decyphered, as I shall be showing, from the actual
message sent on from Washington to Mexico:

19.1.17.

WASHINGTON TO MEXICO
We intended to begin on the first of February unrestricted
submarine warfare. We shall endeavour in spite of this to
keep the USA neutral. In the event of this not succeeding
we make Mexico a proposal of alliance on the following
terms:—

Make war together
Make peace together

Generous financial support and an undertaking on our part
that Mexico is to reconquer the lost territory in Texas, New
Mexico and Arizona. The settlement in detail is left to you.
  You will inform the President of the above most
secretly as soon as the outbreak of war with USA is
certain, and add the suggestion that he should on his own
initiative invite Japan to immediate adherence and at the
same time mediate between Japan and ourselves.

ZIMMERMANN

And reading this completed draft we saw at once that Zimmermann could hardly have used words better calculated on publication to infuriate the people of the United States, and in particular those in the Middle West and Western States, whose outlook on foreign affairs was so largely limited to the potential menaces of Mexico and Japan.

That same day I telephoned to Eddie Bell, for it had always been my intention that at the first possible moment our friends at the American Embassy should share, unofficially, in what was so essentially an 'American secret'. Within half an hour he was in my room. I gave him a copy of the Bernstorff-Eckardt message to read, and I have rarely seen a man blow off steam in so forthright a manner. He was furious.

Mexico to 'reconquer the lost territory'! Texas and Arizona? Why not Illinois and New York while they were about it? But the text was incredible. Might it not be a hoax? It must be a hoax. The Germans had made some pretty bad mistakes in their time, but never before anything like this.

After so many days of anxious waiting I found that I could listen to him with considerable relish.

'But, DID, this means war!' he said at last, when I had assured him that the message was far from being a hoax.

'If it is published, you mean.'

He looked at me. 'If? When Texas and Arizona are to be parcelled off . . . Why, whoever heard of such an insult! DID,' he finished in a lower tone, 'what are you going to do? Are we to be given the cable?'

I explained that the Foreign Office had not yet been able to come to a decision. There were difficulties in our way. Information which I had no objection to giving him privately would have to be given officially to his government. It had still to be settled whether the dispatch should be shown only to the President or given to the American public. 'What I want you to do,' I finished, 'is to tell your Ambassador what you have seen and beg to make no use of the information until Mr Balfour has made his decision.'

'I see. Well, the Ambassador will be mighty grateful to you. We'll sit tight, of course, for as long as you say, but for goodness' sake let us have it as soon as you can.'

I shook hands, and a few minutes later was crossing the Horse Guards Parade on my way to the Foreign Office. For the past week or so I had been seeing Ronald Campbell every day, and we had discussed every possible suggestion, but to every one of them certain objections had been, and were still being, raised. Very properly Lord Hardinge himself was averse from any step which could possibly convey the impression to Washington that there was a *chambre noire* in the Foreign Office or that the British government was endeavouring to influence a neutral State in its favour. Today, as it happened, there was further news from Mexico. United States anxiety was increasing. General Pershing had been ordered to withdraw his troops from Mexican territory, and President Carranza had refused to recognise the right of the United States to interfere in any way in Mexican affairs. He had even ignored Mr Wilson's proposal for a joint policing of the border. In addition there was a fresh rising in the south, where a nephew of Porfirio Diaz was giving trouble. Many German reservists, moreover, were now converging upon Mexico City and attempting to raise a force 'to repel any troops who might be landed from the United States or from Great Britain to safeguard the oil-fields about Tempico.' At the same time the German-Americans in the United States were extremely active in their endeavours to stay the President's hand. I felt that the time had come for immediate action, and formally pressed for a decision.

A day or two later I received the following memorandum:

Foreign Office
February 20, 1917

Lord Hardinge,

In giving me this paper Captain Hall submitted the following considerations:—

Assuming that the Cabinet are anxious for America's entry into the war as a belligerent (a view in which he personally concurs from an Admiralty standpoint), he submits that such a consummation could be hastened by a judicious use of this information. He would suggest that he be authorised to give the substance to Mr. Bell of the United States Embassy who after informing the Ambassador would see that it reached the President. This might be a better plan than that the information should be given the Ambassador from the Foreign Office, which, even though done quite privately, necessarily has a more formal character and might have the appearance that HM Government were trying to bring America in. Captain Hall has given the Embassy a considerable amount of information useful to them in this way and they place reliance in it. Or, if it be desired to give the matter more publicity and consequently to produce more effect on the American people, for whose unanimity President Wilson is waiting, Captain Hall could arrange for it to come out in the American press without any indication that HM Government or any British official, was at the bottom of the exposure. Whichever plan is adopted, Captain Hall is confident that he can arrange things so as to prevent any risk of the source of his information being compromised. Publication in the American press might create a furore of indignation.

R.H. Campbell

```
It is difficult to say which course would be best, but it
seems to me that it would be difficult to explain to Mr.
Bell how we came to be in possession of this news, and
how to convince him of its authenticity. If it could come
out of the United States press without any indication of
its more recent origin being disclosed this would be a
better course, but great care would be necessary.
```
Hardinge

```
I think Captain Hall may be left to clinch this problem.
He knows the ropes better than anyone.
```
A.J. Balfour

That was good enough. The job had been officially entrusted to the Intelligence Division, and without delay we set to work.

Prolonged discussions with Dr Page and Eddie Bell followed, and one point was soon settled. The Ambassador himself was in no doubt at all about the best method to adopt with regard to the handing over of the telegram itself. The effect on the President's mind, he thought, would be infinitely greater if the document were to be given to him officially by the Foreign Secretary; and this Mr Balfour at once agreed to do. But for me there were still the vexed questions of an absolute cover for 40 OB, the necessity for our doing nothing on American soil to which the American people could object, the possible refusal to accept the genuineness of the message, and finally the steps which would have to be taken in the event of Zimmermann himself denouncing the telegram as a forgery.

So far, however, as 40 OB was concerned, we did seem to be in a fairly safe position if we could be sure that in the eyes of the world the Americans themselves would be held wholly responsible for both the discovery and the exposure of the telegram. And here Eddie Bell was reassuring. The American Secret Service, he thought, would be well able to shoulder all the necessary responsibility, and already I was making it my business to see that they should take all the credit. Luckily, too, our copy of the dispatch had been obtained in Mexico and not in the United States, a place of information which could be kept secret except to the President and his immediate advisers, and once the telegram was in American hands, we should to all appearances be outside the game. There was nothing to prevent the American authorities from obtaining their own copy in the Washington cable office, and the fact that the British government had officially provided a decoded transcript would satisfy them of its genuineness. Unfortunately the same view might not be taken in all quarters, and in that case what could be done? Were we to hand over de Grey's reconstructed code even to a friendly neutral State? I could not see myself taking the risk, and yet how else was proof to be given that we were not clumsy forgers?

And then, all of a sudden, a possible solution suggested itself, and one so simple that I wondered why it had not occurred to any of us before. All future moves were to be wholly American. If, as we hoped, the President decided to expose the telegram, he would be in a position to state that it had been obtained by Americans on American soil. Challenged further, however, he would not be able to guarantee its genuineness without de Grey's reconstructed code, and this must certainly never be allowed out of our hands. But if the President was able to say that the deciphering had also been carried out by Americans on American soil, surely that would be sufficient. And there was one way in which this could be done, for Eddie Bell could be asked to decypher the message sent from Washington under de Grey's tuition and in his own embassy which, technically speaking, was American ground. That, at any rate, was my original idea, and although it was slightly modified when the American government did ask for the code, we were able to make good use of it.

As for Zimmermann's possible denial, it seemed better to wait until after the exposure before taking any decision, for it might well be that the American government would find its own way of dealing with the matter.

After that things happened speedily enough. On Saturday, 24 February, while the newspapers in Washington were asserting that in official circles there was some hope of a real chance of averting trouble, Dr Page called at the Foreign Office and was officially handed the Bernstorff-Eckardt dispatch. He lost no time, and within a few hours two cables were on their way to the State Department:

London

Feb. 24. 1917

In about three hours I shall send a telegram of great
importance to the President and Secretary of State.

PAGE

London

Feb. 24. 1917

Confidential for the President and Secretary of State.
Balfour has handed me the translation of a cypher message
from Zimmermann, the German Secretary of State for
Foreign Affairs, to the German Minister in Mexico, which
was sent via Washington and relayed by Bernstorff on
January 19th.

You can probably obtain a copy of the text relayed by
Bernstorff from the cable office in Washington. The first
group is the number of the telegram. 130, and the second
is 13042, indicating the number of the code used. The
last but two is 97556, which is Zimmermann's signature.

I shall send you by mail a copy of the cypher text and
of the decode into German, and meanwhile I give you the
English translation as follows:

(Here follows the text as printed above)

The receipt of this information has so greatly
exercised the British Government that they have lost
no time in communicating it to me to transmit to you in

order that you might be able, without delay, to make
such dispositions as may be necessary in view of the
threatened invasion of our territory.
The following paragraph is strictly confidential.

Early in the war the British Government obtained
possession of a copy of the German cypher code used in the
above message[3] and have made it their business to obtain
copies of Bernstorff's cypher messages to Mexico, amongst
others, which are sent back to London and decyphered
there. This accounts for their being able to decypher this
message from the German Government to their representative
in Mexico and also for the delay from January 19th until
now in their receiving the information.

This system has hitherto been a jealously guarded secret
and is only divulged now to you by the British Government
in view of the circumstances and their friendly feelings
towards the United States. They earnestly request that
you will keep the source of your information, and the
British Government's method of obtaining it profoundly
secret, but they put no prohibition on the publication of
Zimmermann's Telegram itself.

---

3   This, of course, was not so; but it was the official explanation which we had
     decided to give to the American government. It was thought to be a better
     safeguard for 40 OB than the actual truth. A codebook was always liable to reach
     enemy hands. It might be recovered from a sunken ship or from a Zeppelin
     brought down or even on the field of battle; and the same risk of its loss was
     being taken throughout the war by every one of the belligerents. In the event of
     any leakage it would be much better, from our point of view, for the Germans to
     suppose that a copy of their 13040 codebook had come into our hands than that
     without any such assistance we were able to read their most secret dispatches.

     Actually, I understand, in German official circles it was generally held that we
     had obtained our information from a stolen copy of the decyphered dispatch,
     and this in spite of Magnus's careful explanations.

The copies of this, and other telegrams, were not
obtained in Washington, but were bought in Mexico.
I have thanked Balfour for the service his Government has
rendered us and suggest that a private official message of
thanks from our Government to him would be appreciated.

   I am informed that this information has not yet been given
to the Japanese Government but I think it not unlikely that,
when it reaches them, they will make a public statement on
it in order to clear up their position regarding America
and prove their good faith in their allies.

                                                    PAGE.

After which, I suppose, there came what was for me personally the most
anxious time of the whole war. I had assumed this new responsibility:
would it be justified? Had we done all that was possible to safeguard
Room 40? Even so, was there a chance that the Zimmermann Telegram
would misfire? I was, I admit, dreadfully worried. America's entry into the
war within the next few weeks was of the greatest possible importance
to the Allies. I was, indeed, staking everything upon it. But suppose there
were further delays: suppose something went wrong! Both Dr Page and
Eddie Bell were confident, but I confess that for about three days I lived
in a kind of nightmare. And it was not as if the Zimmermann Telegram
was the only matter which was occupying our attention. As luck would
have it, there was at this time the worrying business at Cartagena with
the buoys, the submarine attack on the Dutch ships which had just
sailed from Falmouth, the sinking of the *Laconia* without warning, and
much work to be done in Cuba, whither the Germans were hurriedly
removing their New York Intelligence Centre.

   On the 28th, however, Dr Page was able to tell me that he had been
instructed to thank Mr Balfour for information 'of such inestimable
value', and that the telegram, which had been duly discovered in the cable
office, would be exposed on 1 March. Apparently all was well, but at a
later hour that day Eddie Bell brought me three other messages, all dated
17 January, from Bernstorff to German Legations in South America,

which had been discovered at the same time, and informed me that the Ambassador had been asked to secure if possible a copy of the codebook and decypher their contents himself. It was further suggested that if the State Department were put in possession of the code, there might be much saving of time and expense.

So, in much the way that we had anticipated, the American government were seeking to guard themselves against any accusation of forgery or hoax. My views, however, remained unchanged. Any decyphering which had to be done must be carried out in London and under our immediate supervision. Privately both the Ambassador and Eddie Bell agreed with me, though officially they felt obliged to press the point. Meanwhile Montgomery, another of our decypherers, who had temporarily taken de Grey's place while he was at work on the new German code, had been given the three messages to decypher, and, after receiving the decoded translations, the Ambassador at once sent off his reply:

March 1, 1917

PAGE TO THE SECRETARY OF STATE
Confidential.
The three messages were decyphered today and are
practically identical. They contain instructions to the
three legations to use a certain variation of the cypher
book when communicating with Berlin.

The question of our having a copy of the code has been
taken up, but there appear to be difficulties. I am told
actual code would be of no use to us as it was never used
straight, but with a great number of variations which
are known to only one or two experts here. They cannot
be spared to go to America. If you will send me copies of
B's cypher telegrams the British authorities will gladly
decypher them as quickly as possible, giving me copies as
fast as decyphered. I could telegraph texts or summaries in
matters of importance and send the others by pouch. Neither
Spring Rice nor Gaunt knows anything about this matter.

PAGE

By this time the telegram had actually been published in New York and created, as we hoped and expected, the most tremendous sensation. It had not, however, in the first instance been issued on the authority of the State Department, but as a dispatch of the Associated Press, and almost at once suspicions had been roused in various quarters – some of them, as I shall be showing, most influential. The American government therefore fell in with my suggestion that Eddie Bell be allowed personally to decode the Bernstorff-Eckardt dispatch, and that evening cabled instructions to this effect. But it was not considered necessary to have the actual decoding carried out at the embassy, the State Department would be satisfied to be able to announce that the message had been secured 'from its own people', and so it was arranged for Bell to come to my room at the Admiralty.

And there in the presence of de Grey, Serocold and myself, an American citizen deciphered for himself the message as received from his own government.

President Wilson had demanded that the entire German text so obtained should be sent to him, and this Dr Page did in one of his carefully prepared dispatches. But Eddie Bell himself was satisfied with one very short sentence, when the last group had been deciphered, he looked up from his table.

'That's torn it,' said he, and he spoke the truth.

There could, indeed, be no question at all about the effect of the disclosure in the United States. *The Times* fitly summed up the position when it declared that it had 'aroused the public more than anything since the outbreak of war'. And although the method adopted of allowing the Washington correspondent of the Associated Press to be first in the field was open to some objection, his judicious commentary undoubtedly helped to bring about the sudden increase in anti-German feeling that followed.

'The document,' he wrote:

```
supplies the missing link to many separate chains of
circumstances, which until now have seemed to lead to no
```

definite point. It sheds new light upon the frequently
reported, but indefinable, movements of the Mexican
government to couple its situation with the friction
between the United States and Japan.

It gives new credence to persistent reports of
submarine bases on Mexican territory in the Gulf of
Mexico; it takes cognisance of the fact long recognised
by the American Army chiefs, that if Japan ever undertook
to invade the United States it probably would be through
Mexico over the border and into the Mississippi valley to
split the country in two.

It recalls that Count Bernstorff, when handed his
passports, was very reluctant to return to Germany, but
expressed preference for asylum in Cuba. It gives a new
explanation of the repeated arrests on the border of
men charged by American military authorities with being
German intelligence agents.

Last of all, it seems to show a connection with General
Carranza's recent proposal to neutrals that exports of
food and munitions to the *entente* allies be cut off, and
an intimation that he might stop the supply of oil, so
vital to the British navy, which is exported from the
Tampico fields.

The American government, moreover, had most skilfully timed the
exposure for the very day on which a Bill was before the Senate for
giving the President more extensive powers. Naturally in pro-German
quarters the telegram was immediately denounced as a forgery, and a
number of their newspapers made statements for which their editors
must have been exceedingly sorry only a day or two later. In Congress
itself, too, doubts were raised, and a resolution was passed that the
President be asked to state the source of his information. He replied the
same evening through his Secretary of State:

```
Government is in possession of evidence which established
the fact that the note referred to is authentic, and
that it is in possession of the United States, and that
the evidence was procured by this Government during the
past week, but that it is in my opinion incompatible with
public interest to send to the Senate at the present
time, any further information in possession of the
Government of the United States relative to the note
mentioned in the resolution of the Senate.
                                      ROBERT LANSING
```

This utterly disconcerted the pro-German press, and most of these newspapers were forced to recant. Yet in private the word 'forgery' was still being freely used, and it continued to be used until late on the Friday evening, 2 March, the German official wireless contained Zimmermann's frank admission that this note was genuine.

```
                                        New York
                                     6 March, 1917
GAUNT TO HALL
On the Friday night March 2nd I was the guest of the
'Round Table', which of course is the hottest stuff in New
York in that line: it contains of about thirty members,
and about eighteen attended. Choate was in the chair, and
Root, Wickersham, Olin, Milburn and other men of that
type were in the party. After dinner they all drew their
chairs up round the fire and went for me. Choate openly
said that the Zimmermann note was a forgery, and was
practically unanimously supported by the whole bunch. I
pointed out that both the President and his right hand
man had given their word that they knew it was not, and
that it should be accepted as genuine. Choate then said
that he thought a committee of Congressmen and Senators
should be given the proofs, and I stuck to it that it
would be most unwise where men's lives were involved to
```

give any details to men like Stone, Follette, O'Gorman, etc., and that turned the tide in my favour. They had to admit that I was right. Root then turned to me and asked me if I was satisfied that it was a genuine thing and at the same time Choate asked me point blank whether I knew anything about it. I objected to the latter question, but as my reply left them fairly convinced that I did know, I then told them that information had been conveyed to me by US authorities, that I was satisfied that the note was correct, and a little surprised that they should cross-examine me on it instead of accepting the word of their President. That carried the day completely. The above is an illustration of the way it was received over here, nineteen out of twenty men believed it was a forgery, and had not Zimmermann come out with his statement on Saturday, I think it would have done us a great deal of harm. As it was, it was a complete success, because Viereck, Ritter, and all the rest of the inkslingers just had time to get their yarn into the papers, pointing how obviously it was a British fake, when Zimmermann's statement knocked the bottom out of everything.

German Official Wireless, March 2
The American Press contains reports about instructions from the Ministry for Foreign Affairs to the German Minister at Mexico City in case Germany after the proclamation of unrestricted submarine warfare should fail to keep the United States neutral.

These reports are based on the following facts:

After the decision had been taken to begin unrestricted submarine warfare on February 1, we had, in view of the previous attitude of the American Government, to reckon with the possibility of a conflict with the United States. That this calculation was right is proved by facts, because the American Government severed diplomatic relations with

THE ZIMMERMANN TELEGRAM . . .

```
Germany soon after the proclamation of the barred zone and
asked other neutrals to join in this demarche.
    Anticipating these possibilities, it was not only
the right but the duty of our Government to take
precautions in time, in the event of a warlike conflict
with the United States, in order to balance if possible
the adhesion of our enemies to a new enemy. The German
Minister in Mexico was therefore, in the middle of
January, instructed should the United States declare
war, to offer the Mexican Government an alliance and to
arrange further details.
    These instructions, by the way, expressly enjoined the
Minister to make no advances to the Mexican Government
unless he knew for a certainty that America was going
to declare war. How the American Government received
information of instructions sent by a secret way to
Mexico is not known, but it appears that treachery (and
this can only be the case) has been committed on American
territory.
```

So far so good. When during the subsequent debate in the Senate on the Armed Neutrality Bill, only thirteen opponents could be found, we felt fairly confident. True, this 'little group of wilful men', to use the President's own words, were able to talk out the measure, but the feeling of the American nation as a whole had been shown in no uncertain manner. War was inevitable. But to us in the ID there was still the question: had we fully safeguarded Room 40? Obviously the Germans would make the most strenuous efforts to discover the truth: how near to it were they likely to get?

Now Zimmermann's speedily published admission was by no means the stupid move that some people held it to be. As yet he had no definite information with regard to the 'treachery', but he was not to be blamed for believing that it had been committed on American territory, and he knew that a denial would only mean the production of the original telegram, and possibly others with it, from the Washington cable office. And if a copy of their codebook had been found, he would be helpless. He took what in my opinion was the wisest course, though it led to his downfall. What steps, however, would he be likely to take to discover the leak? And, in the first place, how far, if at all, would 13040 seem to be compromised if the original German text of his telegram remained unpublished? Clearly it was important from our point of view to prevent its publication, and this we were able to do:

```
                                              London
                                        March 10, 1917
PAGE TO LANSING
The authorities directly concerned would prefer that the
German text should not be published, as its publication
in entirety would indicate that our Government or some
other parties are able to decypher the German code used
in its transmission from Washington to Mexico and the
Germans would then cease using it elsewhere. This is
information which, judging by Zimmermann's reported
statements, they do not now possess and a confirmation of
what they may suspect would be of great value to them.
At present the Germans cannot know exactly where or
how the leak occurred; for all they know a copy of the
message may have been lost or removed from the German
Embassy in Washington, or the leak might have occurred
between Berlin and Washington.
   Were serious doubts being cast in America on the
genuineness of the instructions to the German Minister
in Mexico the authorities here might reconsider
their position, but as Zimmermann has admitted their
genuineness in the Reichstag this can hardly be the case.
```

At the same time neither American assumption of responsibility nor American courtesy to ourselves could completely exonerate us in

German eyes. In the Senate debate of 1 March Mr Stone and others had not hesitated to speak of the telegram as 'in all probability a forgery by the British Secret Service', and similar statements had appeared in many of the American newspapers. True, these had soon given place to other statements, prompted in some cases, I must admit, by Gaunt or myself, in which the surprisingly good work of the American Secret Service was held up as a model for all the world; but we were not yet clear of the business, and the utmost caution was still necessary.

I have seen it stated in various accounts that an extremely virulent attack on the Intelligence Division appeared in the *Daily Mail* during the first week in March. Therein, it is stated, the most unfavourable comparison was drawn between our own Intelligence Service and that of the Americans, who without any of our war experience to guide them, had been able with startling rapidity to lay bare a vast conspiracy against them. It is also said that this newspaper attack had been engineered by myself as part of a campaign to mislead the Germans.

In point of actual fact no such article appeared, either in the *Daily Mail* or in any other British newspaper. On the other hand its quite true that my old friend Thomas Marlowe, the then editor of the *Daily Mail*, and I did discuss the possibility of publishing some attack on the ID, and, so far as I recollect, a rough draft was drawn up and may conceivably be still in existence. Afterwards, however, it was considered inadvisable to print any such article in a British newspaper at a time when there was such great public anxiety about the German submarines and so soon after the Board of Admiralty had been reconstituted.

And looking back to those days I cannot help smiling at some of the tall stories about the acquisition of the telegram which I was at some pains not to contradict. Secret codes, it was hinted, had been stolen in the unlikeliest places and bought by the Americans for the most colossal sums. Heroic backwoodsmen from Arizona searching for excitement in France had broken through the enemy line disguised as Church Army padres, obtained jobs in Brussels, discovered 'the German cypher-book' in the governor-general's own house, and hurried back with the precious code to astounded officials in Washington. There were weird stories of German submarine captains being robbed on Broadway and Mexican revolutionaries who had captured wireless stations which never existed, and even one of a German agent in New York who after witnessing the piratical exploits of *U.53* had forthwith seen the error of his ways, obtained American citizenship, and with the help of the notorious Graves, recently accused of blackmailing Countess Bernstorff, successfully burgled the German embassy.

With the American journalists in London, too, I had no little fun. Recent reports from New York had warned us that the Swedish Minister at Washington was playing a somewhat similar game to Cronholm's, and about this time, as it happened, we had obtained possession of a trunk of his on board the *Frederick VIII* on its way to Europe. The Foreign Office was inclined to accept the Swedish Minister's statement that it contained only diplomatic correspondence but I had pointed out that this statement was inconclusive inasmuch as the diplomatic correspondence might not be exclusively Swedish. Which, we had discovered, it was not. The American journalists over here had got hold of the story and were eager for details. 'They are quite convinced,' I wrote to Gaunt on 22 March, 'that the American Secret Service abstracted the Zimmermann Telegram from the trunk which was taken out of the *Frederick VIII*. They tackled me yesterday about it, and I had to admit that all the evidence pointed to the seals having been broken before we took the chest. It is a very safe line, and I think I will stick to it.'

The circulation of such stories had, of course, no effect on the Germans' endeavour to discover the truth, but as they continued to make use of 13040, though warned that it might be compromised, we were able to follow each move.

On the day of the disclosure, the *Universal*, a pro-Ally Mexican paper, had reproduced the Washington message, and Eckardt had promptly cabled home:

```
                                    Mexico, Mar. 1.
Of course I did not make the communication here.
Treachery or indiscretion here out of the question;
therefore apparently it happened in the USA, or cypher
13040 is compromised ... I denied everything here.
```

Berlin naturally required further details. Not all German newspapers were too eager on this occasion to fall into line, and the *Frankfurter Zeitung* was only one of many to demand much fuller explanations than those already given. 'The statement,' declared this newspaper on 5 March, 'that our former Ambassador Count Bernstorff had intended to transmit the cable which he had received from Berlin in autograph copy and by special messenger to the German Legation in Mexico, but that the document had somehow been extracted from the special courier, need not be accepted without further proof.' But what was the truth?

Undoubtedly there has been some trickery, but how the American Government got hold of the compromising document they are not likely to tell us. In any case it remains highly regrettable that the German service does not dispose of the necessary facilities to ensure the safe transmission of such an important document to its proper destination. Such incidents may do very serious harm to our Foreign policy. One must say quite frankly that in such a case the proper guarding of the secret was the most important aspect of the whole enterprise.

For some little while we remained in ignorance of the precise steps which Berlin was taking, but before the end of the month we had news enough:

```
                                         No. 20
                                21st March, 1917

BERLIN TO MEXICO
Most secret. Decypher personally.
Please cable in same cypher who decyphered Cable
```

Dispatches 1 and 2 [i.e. Zimmermann's two telegrams of Jan 16th and Feb 7th] how the originals and decodes were kept, and, in particular, whether both dispatches were kept in the same place.

STUMM

A few days later it seemed as though the Germans might be getting nearer to the truth:

No. 20
21st March, 1917

BERLIN TO MEXICO
Various indications suggest that treachery was committed in Mexico.
The greatest caution is indicated.
Burn all compromising material.

Eckardt's replies showed his state of mind, and indeed he and Magnus were now in a very difficult position:

21st March, 1917

ECKARDT TO ZIMMERMANN
Both dispatches were decyphered, in accordance with my special instructions, by Magnus. Both, as is the case with everything of a politically secret nature, were kept from the knowledge of the Chancery officials.

Telegram No 1 was received here in cypher 13040, while Kinkel who is at present employed here in Berlin, previously employed in our Embassy in Washington, thinks he remembers that it was sent off by the Washington Embassy, like all telegrams sent here in cypher, from Cape Cod.

The originals in both cases were burned by Magnus and the ashes scattered. Both dispatches were kept in an absolutely secure steel safe, procured especially for

the purpose and installed in the Chancery building, in
Magnus's bedroom, up to the time when they were burned.

ECKARDT

30th March, 1917
ECKARDT TO ZIMMERMANN
Reply to telegram No 22 Greater caution than is always
exercised here would be impossible. The text of the
telegrams which have arrived is read to me at night in my
dwelling house by Magnus in a low voice. My servant, who
does not understand German, sleeps in an annexe. Apart
from this, the text is never anywhere but in Magnus's
hand or in the steel safe, the method of opening which is
known only to him and myself.

According to Kinkel, in Washington even secret
telegrams were known to the whole Chancery. Two copies
were regularly made for the Embassy records. Here there
can be no question of carbon copies or waste paper.

Please inform me at once, as soon as we are exculpated,
as we doubtless shall be; otherwise, I insist, as does
Magnus also, on a judicial investigation, if necessary,
by Consul Grunow.

And this pathetic communication had the desired effect:

4th April, 1917
BERLIN TO MEXICO
After your telegram it is hardly conceivable that
betrayal took place in Mexico. In face of it the
indications which point in that direction lose their
force. No blame rests on either you or Magnus.

FOREIGN OFFICE

Berlin was right. Who could have taken better precautions than the obese
Magnus with his steel safe and his low voice and his careful burning of

the ashes? Obviously the theft had taken place in Washington. Equally obviously the American Secret Service was highly efficient.

We began to breathe freely.

Meanwhile the Germans were continuing their negotiations with Mexico, and much to our surprise, using 13040 for the purpose. As each of their telegrams was intercepted and decoded, a copy was handed to the American Embassy to be forwarded on to Washington. For a little while it seemed possible that Carranza would join forces with the enemy, but he had been angered by the publication of the Zimmermann Telegram, and Japan had shown clearly enough what she thought about it, and once the United States had taken the final step, he decided to remain 'strictly neutral'.

There is no need for me to say much more on this matter. By the 19th the newspapers were reporting that the position in the States was 'tantamount to a state of war'. Three days later it was learnt that the President had summoned Congress to meet on 2 April.

Congress duly met, and in the course of his speech Mr Wilson mentioned that the intrigues of the German government had 'played their part in serving to convince us at last that that Government entertains no real friendship for us, and means to act against our peace and security at its convenience. That it seems to stir up enemies against us,' he continued, 'at our very doors, the intercepted Note to the German Minister at Mexico City is eloquent evidence.'

At a little after one o'clock on the afternoon of the 6th he signed the Declaration of War.

That evening de Grey and myself drank champagne.

COMMENTARY ON HALL'S CHAPTERS AND GAZETTEER

Chapter 1: 'The Nature of Intelligence Work'

This eleven-page chapter is written with lucidity and highlights key points in intelligence work. It starts with a commentary on novelists who 'romanticise' intelligence work and on those who, like Somerset Maugham, Temple Thurston and A.E.W. Mason, write from first-hand experience. Maugham (1874–1965) was the highest paid author of the 1930s. Invited into the SIS in 1916 he was tasked with keeping the Bolsheviks in the war but said later that he was sent in six months too late. His book *Ashenden or the British Agent* includes real life stories of the world of spies. Ian Fleming is said to have been influenced by this book.

Temple Thurston (1879–1933) was an Anglo-Irish playwright and author of forty books. *Portrait of a Spy*, 1929, is an account of a French female spy prior to and during the First World War. A.E.W. Mason (1865–1948) was a prolific writer of detective and adventure novels, some based on his work as a secret agent in Spain and Morocco as part of the Thoroton Network (*The Winding Stair* of 1923 is the best fictional example we have) and later in Mexico.

Ian Fleming's James Bond is certainly anticipated in Hall's reference to 'blonde ladies'. Fleming (1908–1964) was, as everyone knows, the creator of James Bond. Coming from a wealthy banking family, Robert Fleming & Co., he was assistant to Rear Admiral John Godfrey (DNI). He planned many secret service actions, including Operation GOLDENEYE and Operation RUTHLESS, and he set up a counter Nazi operation in Spain in the event of the Nazis invading that country. He helped initiate the Office of Strategic Services (OSS), which became the CIA.

Even SIS memoires offer only half the truth, as no one can give anything like a complete picture, including Hall himself. Hall's biography is about a single department and not many spies figure in the text. However, sheer fantastic improbabilities make for extraordinary reading, as exemplified by the account of the sinking of *U-28*. Launched in 1913, she had sunk thirty-nine ships: 93,782 tons of shipping. She was herself sunk in the Arctic Sea in 1917 during an attack on the SS *Olive Branch*, an armed English steamer.

This chapter describes how a minor naval department grew into one with worldwide commitments and Hall attributes this largely to a wonderful, heterogeneous staff.[1] It had its successes and its failures, the successes far outweighing the failures. Hall writes of financiers, novelists and 'stupid sportsmen', and others, as being part of his heterogeneous staff.

Hall lists four cardinal points: 1. Acquisition of information about the enemy; 2. Sifting and knitting this together to provide a balanced picture; 3. How to use the information; 4. The need to cover all your tracks so that the enemy remains in ignorance. These points need to be examined against present day practice but this writer suspects that Point 2 is perhaps more difficult to achieve today, due to the massive stream of intelligence traffic generated in the computer and satellite age. Point 4 may also be more difficult due to satellite intervention,

---

1   See maps 2 and 3.

electronic communications hacking and other such factors such as drones and social communication. This, clearly, is a subject about which only the most leading secret intelligence experts can make a comment.

He emphasises how secret information is vulnerable to disclosure, calling for careful 'need to know' criteria, and how important it is to retain a small, decentralised staff to help to ensure this. The importance of contributions and ideas 'coming from the bottom up' cannot be overemphasised.

Emerging seemingly unrelated and trivial facts can often finally link up with other information and enable the jigsaw to be completed. (This is an important theme of R. V. James in his *Most Secret War*). By contrast, much 'outside information', that is information coming in from people not actually involved in intelligence (he examples Sir Marcus Samuel and Sir Henri Deterding, both outstanding figures in their own right, along with Mr Colyn) was relatively worthless, only two or three outside sources proving to be of any value. A brief note on two of these men is justified here since their worldwide roles were so important in economic, commercial, military and political issues. Sir Marcus Samuel (1853–1927) was afterwards 1st Viscount Bearstead, founder of Shell Transport & Trading Company, precursor of Royal Dutch Shell. A visit to the Black Sea in 1890 had opened his eyes to the importance of oil and he ordered the construction of eight tankers. His family were Far East traders and he was himself a financial genius. Sir Henri Deterding (1866–1939) bought the Azerbaijan oil fields from the Rothschilds in 1911. He created the Royal Dutch Petroleum Co. and became chairman of Royal Dutch Shell. As an admirer of the Nazis in 1936 he gave 1 million Reichsmarks to Hitler and other donations to the Nazi Party. Forced to resign he moved to Germany and died in Switzerland.

Colyn (actually spelt Colijn, 1869–1944) was a brutal suppressor of native peoples in the Dutch East Indies, 1893–1909. He was Prime Minister of the Netherlands in 1925–26 and 1933–39. He responded to the Great Depression with an austere economic policy. He gave the Kaiser refuge after the First World War and in 1940 advocated German leadership in Europe. Then turning to political resistance he was arrested but Himmler kept him as a bargaining pawn and held him under house arrest in Germany where he died in custody in 1944.

Hall writes at some length on deception plans, exampling the Kiel Regatta of 1909: 'innocent activity' as a cover for intelligence gathering, an echo of *The Riddle of the Sands*.[2] Britain at that time was concerned over German naval construction but uncovering it was achieved, finally, through Hall's inventive and unconventional methods. The incident of the Dutch spy (later shot) is an example of how Hall would investigate any report, irrespective of whichever source it came from. The young naval friend, recounting his experiences in the Red Sea, 'unwittingly helped to put us in possession of a much wanted copy of the German Foreign Office cypher-book'. This almost certainly relates to Wassmuss, said to be the model for the German agent in John Buchan's *Greenmantle* where his character Bullivant is said to have been modelled on Hall. Wilhem Wassmuss (1890–1931) was a German diplomat fermenting trouble in the Persian Gulf in the First World War. He spread his network from Iran to Afghanistan and India. The period 1909–19 saw the 'Wassmuss Chaos' leading to the death of 8–9 million Iranians and the Armenian Genocide with 1.5 million deaths. He organised five 'rebel' groups and precipitated sixteen assassinations and acts of terror in Persia. Britain offered a £500,000 reward for his capture. Escaping from captivity just before the arrival of the British, he left his luggage behind. This included the German diplomatic codebook which found its way to the India Office. Hall's inspiration led Cozens-Hardy to the India Office and the codebook passed into Room 40's hands. Wassmuss died forgotten and in poverty in Berlin. Reverting to Hall's first intelligence mission in Kiel Harbour in 1908, German precautions were particularly effective for their submarine programme. The first German experimental submarine had been launched in 1850. It was unsuccessful and sank. By 1903 they completed the *Forelle*, their first fully functional U-Boat. The first U-Boats were commissioned in 1906. Hall was not directed to U-Boat construction as this was not known about by the Admiralty. In July 1914, Admiral Sir Barry Domville (DNI, 1927 to

---

2   See map 4.

1930) dismissed the threat of U–Boats attacking merchant shipping. By 1930 Domville espoused the Nazi cause, was denounced by the Lords Selbourne, Walter and Grenfell and interned in Brixton Prison in 1940.

John Buchan (1875–1940), 1st Baron Tweedsmuir, was Director of Information from 1917 and worked with Hall and Sir Basil Thomson. He was the author of over fifty books, many featuring fast-moving adventure stories, *Prester John* and counter-espionage classic *The Thirty-Nine Steps* being good examples. He was made Governor-General of Canada in 1935 and died there five years later. He knew Hall well.

Hall's department had 'no executive functions' and, as secret information was very vulnerable, he wrote that 'Silence where Possible' was the best motto that could be adopted.

His paragraph starting, 'Luckily in the matter of information …' is annotated, possibly by Ralph Straus (1882–1991). Educated at Harrow and Pembroke College, Cambridge, he specialised in Charles Dickens and the early printers and inventors of print type. He was also a prolific novelist and biographer. His papers are held by Georgetown University. In this chapter Straus commented that it needed to be toned down in respect of the volume of enemy code messages being intercepted 'towards the end of the war'. This is the only amendment made to the text.

The following notes relate to other personalities and ships and boats which figure in Hall's Chapter 1 but which are not referred to in the commentary. While most if not all of these names would have been familiar to Hall's contemporaries they are largely unknown nearly 100 years on. They are placed here in alphabetical order for ease of reference. Page numbers are included which refer to Hall's manuscript.

Gazetteer
BLÜCHER, German armoured cruiser, 1909, 15,842 tons. Sunk at the Battle of the Dogger Bank in 1915 by gunfire from Beatty's battle squadron. Crew rescues by a British destroyer were rendered impossible by a Zeppelin bombing the destroyer, thinking that the *Blücher* was a British battleship. Only 234 men survived out of a complement of 1,200. (p. 35)

VICE ADMIRAL SIR FRANCIS BRIDGEMAN GCB GCVO (1848–1929). As First Sea Lord he clashed with Churchill on technical and traditional naval procedures leading to his resignation. A gunnery officer, amongst his qualities was the ability to delegate, rare in the Royal Navy of those days. (p. 31)

HMS *CORNWALL* was a Monmouth-class armoured cruiser and a Cadet Training ship 1908-1909. In 1914 she took part in the Battle of the Falklands and was in the final chase of the *Leipzig* which she set on fire. *Leipzig* rolled over and sank, leaving only thirteen survivors. (p. 31)

JOHN FISHER, 1ST BARON FISHER (1841–1920). Said to be the greatest Admiral after Nelson. First Sea Lord, 1904, he reorganised the fleet and dockyard management; developed the submarine; improved the gunnery; and converted from coal to oil power. Renowned for his development of the Dreadnoughts, he resigned in 1915 as a protest against Churchill's Dardanelles campaign. As a result Churchill too had to resign, whereupon he joined in the trench warfare in France as lieutenant colonel commanding the 6th Battalion, Royal Scots Fusiliers. For the rest of the war Fisher served on the Board of Innovations. (p. 35)

GRIANAIG. Twin-screw schooner, she is described as 'a classic gentleman's yacht'. (p. 32)

PRINCE HENRY OF PRUSSIA (1862–1929). Son of Emperor Frederick III and Victoria, Princess Royal, eldest daughter of Queen Victoria. By 1906 he was commander of the High Seas Fleet and in 1909 promoted to grand admiral. As C-in-C Baltic Fleet in 1914 he held the Russian naval forces at bay, preventing their attack on the German coast. Popular and diplomatic, he was open and humble of manner. He was chief patron of the Yacht Club of Kiel, 1887, of which he was one of its founders. He introduced submarines and aircraft into the German navy. (p. 32)

GRAND ADMIRAL ALFRED VON TIRPITZ (1849–1930). With the so-called Tirpitz Plans for the development of the German Imperial Navy he alarmed Great Britain. In the 1890s he took the modest German Navy into a world-class force. After Jutland he turned to submarine warfare but was dismissed in 1916. He sent his daughter to Cheltenham Ladies' College. The battleship named after him was sunk by RAF bombers in a Norwegian fjord in 1944. (p. 32)

URSULA, 'A fine racing boat', 50ft in length, won races at Monte Carlo, but an exploding exhaust joint led to her giving up in the ninth round of the 1911 Coup des Nations. (p. 32)

DUKE OF WESTMINSTER, 2nd Duke (1879–1953), known as 'Bendor'. Competed in motor boat races for Great Britain in the London Olympics. His yacht was the *Grianaig* and his motorboat the *Ursula*. He served with distinction in the First World War and developed the armoured car. He later espoused the Nazis and fell out with Churchill. (p. 32)

Chapter 2: Intelligence in Wartime

This is one of the most important chapters available to us. That it is partly in the form of notes shows that the final, non-existent, version (if the chapter was ever finally completed, which is doubtful) would have contained much more specific information. The significance of this chapter is also important in that it gives virtually the overall ethos under which Hall's agents worked.

There would seem to be ten basic themes which emerge, viz.:

1. Tracking ship movements by directional wireless and decyphering

2. Use of information from the world of insurance and re-insurance. Most German insurance was effected in Switzerland. This gave information on German manufacturers

3. Use of agents for government yards that yielded a complete list of all shipbuilding. Agents as a prime source on enemy morale, pinpointing weak points to be exploited by blockade

4. The importance of neutral countries, primarily for information-gathering by agents

5. Action by agents against sabotage, enemy spy rings, money transfers, communication facilities and for obtaining enemy war plans

6. Recuperation of cyphers and codebooks. Advice on not buying enemy cyphers, advantages of planting false cyphers on the enemy

7. Planting of false information in newspapers and deception planning. Plus, obtaining diplomatic papers from the enemy. Leave enemy agents in place and read all their messages

8. The virtue of patience

9. Confidence is vital in building up an operation: never let people down; trust is essential. Lines of communication should never be put at risk

10. Propaganda: Hall lists four purposes and two organisational elements

A close study of these ten points reveals some of the ingredients of Hall's phenomenal success. As well as patience he emphasises the moral qualities: integrity, reliability, sound leadership and delegation.

However it has been said that Hall did not always preserve the highest moral standards. In wartime, in the field of disinformation and black propaganda, the highest moral standards are inevitably subservient to force of circumstance, but in peacetime such activity might be rightly said to contravene aspects of high moral qualities. This is exampled in the Casement affair, where O'Halpin argues that Hall 'allowed himself an outrageous freedom of action' in circulating lurid extracts from Casement's diaries and again later when he told Casement, 'It's better that a cankering sore ... should be cut out'.[3] The Home Office was also implicated when it refused Casement's plea to contact the leaders of the Easter Rising in an effort to stop it. While this can be seen as a case of protecting British interests, Hall was also involved in a more serious affair pertaining to the Zinoviev letter on which different opinions were held as to its authenticity. Hall is said to have forwarded a letter to the *Daily Mail*, signed by Grigori Zinoviev (1883–1936), in an effort to discredit the government at the time of the 1924 elections in order to destroy Labour's chances by portraying it as 'soft on Bolshevism'. This forged letter was attributed, by Great Britain, to having been sent by Zinoviev to inspire increased communist agitation in the country. The forgery was initiated to help swing the popular vote to the advantage of the Conservative Party. Hall is held responsible for effecting this manoeuvre. Zinoviev was Head of the Executive Committee of the Comintern. His execution by Stalin, following a show trial, shocked the world and initiated the Red Terror. He was formally absolved by the Soviet Supreme Court in 1988. Robin Cook commissioned an inquiry in 1998 which confirmed its status as a forgery, which Zinoviev had always maintained.

When in March 1936 Hall addressed the Naval College at Greenwich on 'Intelligence in Wartime' he was speaking to a large audience including members of the Foreign Office and representatives of all three services. He listed four guiding principles: acquisition of information concerning the enemy; sifting this for truth and falsehood; decisions concerning the usage of this information; and the need to cover one's tracks and so prevent the enemy from finding out how this information was obtained. He also listed four propaganda principles: the need to deceive the enemy so he takes a course of

---

3   Euna O'Halpin, *British Intelligence in Ireland 1914–1921*; ref: C.M. Andrew and
     D.N. Dilks.

action detrimental to the enemy's own interests; destabilising enemy morale, particularly amongst civilians; influencing neutral nations in favour of the Allied cause; and warnings to other nations on the risk to them should the enemy win.

Operations MINCEMEAT and FORTITUDE in the Second World War are more recent examples, the first showing that Sardinia and Greece were the targets for the Allies rather than Sicily, the intended target; the second that D-Day would happen in the Pas de Calais and not in Normandy. FORTITUDE even misled Hitler himself.

Returning to Hall's ten themes, with respect to point 6 the *Magdeburg* is very relevant. She was a German lightweight cruiser which ran aground off the coast of Russian Estonia in the early days of the war. Its confidential papers were recovered by the Russians who passed them to Churchill at the Admiralty. This led to the first operational victory of Room 40.

Points 7 and 9 concern the idea of allowing enemy agents to remain in place so that their communication lines remain operative at the time the SIS was reading all their encrypted messages. This happened with Shyam Sundar Chakravarty (1869–1932), the Bengali revolutionary and journalist who was deported to Burma in 1908. Later he was involved in the non-cooperative movement with Mahatma Ghandi. Poison phials containing anthrax and glanders germs were landed by *U-35* (one of four submarines associated with the sinking of the *Lusitania*) in Cartagena harbour, Spain, in 1917.[4] This is an example of keeping information under wraps until the right moment arises.

Lord 'Dick' Herschell was a Commander RNVR, 2nd Baron, and was PA to Hall and head of the Diplomatic Section of Room 40 with special responsibility for Spain and Spanish Latin America. He informed King Alfonso XIII at the right time to ensure the dismissal of Ratibor (1856–1924), the aged and aristocratic prince, German Ambassador to Mexico. Deeply involved in the *Erri*

---

4   See also Stephen Jay Gould, *The Lying Stones of Marrakech*, which gives considerable information on this subject.

Berro wolfram smuggling project Ratibor was expelled from Spain for spying and meddling in politics. He was a vindictive, imperious and lazy individual.

King Alfonso XIII (1886–1941) kept Spain neutral in the First World War as he had relatives on both sides of the conflict. His main later interests were setting up the Paradores Hotels and patronising Spanish football. He abdicated in 1941 and died in Rome the same year.

Hall's important point 9 is exampled by Talaat Bey Pasha (1874–1921), Grand Vizier and Controller of the Ottoman Empire in the Triumvirate called the Three Pashas. He was assassinated in Berlin for his role in the Armenian Genocide. In 1918 he had escaped by submarine from Constantinople and was tracked by British Intelligence. He stands as a classic example of a once valued helper being lost through his loss of confidence in the SIS. By this time Turkey was dying and unable to hold onto the Ottoman Empire it had inherited.

By way of conclusion we now review the remaining people and ships referred to in Hall's Chapter 2.

Gazetteer

THE *BRISTOL* was a light cruiser, launched 1910. She operated in the Falklands, the Mediterranean and off South America. She was the first Royal Navy ship to see action, attacking the German raider *Karlsruhe* in the West Indies in 1914. Her involvement with the *Möwe* is used as an example of 'close reading' and 'understanding what the natural deductions are'. (p. 42)

CARTAGENA. This Murcian port in south-west Spain figures significantly in Room 40's Spanish affairs. The *U-39* sank 155 ships of 407,123 tons, along with one warship, and had taken prizes of 798 tons, all in the Mediterranean. In May 1918 she was interned in Cartagena having been damaged by Allied action. She was surrendered to France and broken up in 1923. (p. 41)

THE *MÖWE* was a German merchant raider and minelayer. The most successful German raider in both world wars she sank the *King Edward VII* near Scapa Flow and the SS *Mount Temple* with 700 horses on board, bound for

France. She captured or sank forty-three ships of 180,000 gross tonnage, mainly British plus three French, two Spanish and one Japanese. Sunk by Beaufighters of Coastal Command during the Second World War. (p. 42).

THE ST JAMES' CLUB has some later association with James Bond, Agent 007, as it was during the Second World War that Ian Fleming lived there for a short while. All the James Bond books, from *Casino Royale* in 1953 to *Octopussy* in 1966, were written in Jamaica. (p. 44)

ARTHUR ZIMMERMANN (1864–1940), Foreign Secretary of the German Empire; his story is told in Chapter 25. Andrew Marr (in his *History of the World*) describes him as 'arguably the most destructive person of the twentieth century'. He assisted the Bolsheviks to undermine the Tsar and sent Lenin into Russia in the infamous 'sealed train', thus contributing to the October Revolution and the rise of international Communism. He fermented trouble in Ireland and with the rebels in India. He supported Francisco Villa and the return of much of Mexico's lost territory from pre-1836 including Texas, New Mexico, Arizona and California. (p. 39)

Chapter 3: A Private Censorship

The chapter starts with an important note, 'Seen by Sir John Cockerill'. Brigadier General Sir George Kynston Cockerill, CB (1867–1957), was a remarkable man. He served in the Hazara Expedition, explored the Hindu Kush, served with the Central Relief Force and as a Staff Officer in the Boer War. In the First World War he was sub director of Military Operations and deputy director of Military Intelligence.

Hall was prepared to take action even if damaging consequences might arise. Provided he could show that these actions were entirely based on the need for the successful prosecution of the war, 'I would be fairly safe'. This was also to apply to, 'well-meaning gentlemen … who saw no reason … to alter their views on procedures'. He admits that this policy of his would annoy such gentlemen, as indeed it did. He also comments on the fact that he was never given any written Admiralty directives for the DNI although he surmises that some must have existed by the time he moved to Whitehall.

It then goes on to those three vitally important issues which he had identified. These are: first, the need for the censorship of all telegrams, cables and wireless messages. The second issue was a search for secret wireless stations in Great Britain. None were ever found but this provided for some adventures by Churchill who participated enthusiastically in the search. The third issue was the censorship of all incoming, outgoing and transit mails. Initially this was for German and Austrian communications only but was later extended to neutral countries and, finally, all foreign countries. That same day Hall attended lunch 'as usual' with Lord Herschell and Colonel Browning.

Colonel F.H. Browning (known as Freddy) is a slightly enigmatic figure. Director of the Savoy and an initial member of the War Trade Intelligence Department, he had the justifiable reputation of being the ideal man about town and an effective 'fixer' or 'force multiplier'. He was the ideal assistant to Cumming and played a significant role in the reorganisation of the SIS and of the Far Eastern and Siberian agents.

Browning was one of the founders of the National Service League (NSL), of which both Herschell and Hall were members. On Hall describing the proposed censorship plan, 'Freddie' (as Hall calls him here) volunteered, 'two hundred fellows' from the NSL. The NSL was a pressure group founded in 1902 to alert the nation to the inadequacy of the army to fight a European war and proposed national service as the solution. By 1910 it had 60,000 members. Its first president was Lord Raglan, followed by Lord Roberts in 1905. Churchill and Lloyd George expressed support but behind the scenes. At its zenith it employed 400 workers.

Hall placed emphasis on two cardinal points. The first is his insistence on good methods for obtaining information but, even more importantly, how to prevent the enemy from copying them. Secondly, the censorship carried out resulted in a radical shift in the blockade system. 'How and where the Germans were ordering vast quantities of contraband stuff', provided the basis of the first real moves in the economic war. This yielded the vital evidence which would prevent the British Prize Courts refusing to condemn cargoes or ships stopped by the Royal Navy. The smooth co-operation of the, then, Colonel Cockerill also went a long way to ease and facilitate Admiralty and War Office relations. Hall goes so far as to state that, without Cockerill's collaboration, 'the war could not have been won'.

Rear Admiral H.F. Oliver was Director of the Intelligence Division (DID), appointed in August 1913. He is widely recognised as the original creator of what came to be known as Room 40, actually the Naval Intelligence Division at the time. His deputy was Captain Thomas Jackson. As Admiral Sir Thomas Jackson (1868–1945) he became Director of Naval Operations from 1915, when regrettably, he provided incorrect information to Jellicoe when he told him the German fleet was in harbour when it was actually at sea and the Battle of Jutland was about to take place. His narrow-mindedness was augmented by an angry and blusterous disposition. He never grasped the importance of cryptology. He was promoted to vice admiral in 1925.

Oliver had brought in Sir Alfred Ewing to take over responsibility for code-breaking, which represented the most important aspect of the work. By 1914 Oliver was leaving his post as DID, coincidentally with Hall leaving command of HMS *Queen Mary*. Lobbied by Hall's wife, the vacancy fell to Hall to the great pleasure of his former C-in-C, Admiral Beatty.

Hall obtained £500,000 from the Prime Minister, Asquith, to set up what he called the War Trade Intelligence Department (WTID). The bizarre and even comical conditions surrounding this decision by Asquith at the Cabinet meeting in No. 10 are beautifully described. This decision was the turning point in British Secret Intelligence and, as Hall writes, he knew 'that in a little while the ID would be doing work far wider in scope than any Admiralty official even that day would have dared to prophesy'. It is not too much to say that the ID and the WTID saw the birth of the modern, and present day, secret intelligence and espionage service in Great Britain. The date was 1914.

On 12 October 1914 Hall was made Director of Naval Intelligence and Ewing continued to be responsible for code-breaking.

On 8 November 1914 Churchill wrote what is referred to as his 'Charter' for this work:

> All officers of the War Staff, preferably from the ID, should be selected to study all the decoded intercepts, not only current but past, and to compare them continually with what actually took place in order to penetrate the German mind and movements, and make reports. All the intercepts are to be written in a locked book with their decodes, and all other copies are to be collected and burnt. All new messages are to be entered in the book, and the book is only to be handled under direction from C.O.S.
>
> I shall be obliged if Sir Alfred Ewing will associate himself continually with this work.
>
> (Initialled by W.S.C. and F, 8/11/14)

It was also in 1914 that Churchill had written his 'Memorandum', which proposed, 'The new duties ... open ... to the Intelligence Division a large creative and imaginative sphere, and offer opportunities for the highest tactical and strategic ability'. Finally, the practical springboard for Room 40 came with the Russian gift of the German codebook from the *Magdenburg*, 25 August 1914.

The 'War Diary & Logbook', dated November 1914, is the first available written record. In a sentence, under the DNI came censorship, blockade and a worldwide Intelligence Service. Events were moving fast.

What lessons might be learnt from this chapter? Perhaps, perception leading to pragmatism; Hall's initial alertness to the possibility of hidden informers leading to a nil return which turned out subsequently to be a triumph. Contacts and personality; Hall was in contact with a galaxy of talent and his magnetic presence worked to achieve the results he sought. What had started as a censorship drive ended with the institution of an entirely new and vital blockade system and the birth of modern intelligence.

It has to be said that although the blockade was highly successful it resulted in a wave of starvation in Germany. German sources claim 763,000 civilian deaths due to starvation and disease up to December 1918. This figure is disputed by later academic research which comes up with a figure of an estimated 424,000.[5] These losses had a debilitating effect on morale in the trenches. Nevertheless the blockade is recognised as one of the key elements in the Allied victory. Perhaps secret intelligence strategy should look beyond the intended, military results. It has been argued that the extent of civilian suffering in Germany and the Central Powers was a contributory factor in the rise of Hitler. Winning the war was the paramount need but this can lead to losing the peace.

This matter of the long-range implications of the use of secret intelligence is partly anticipated by the situation in the Dardanelles in 1915. Hall's plans to get the Turks out of the war, by spending up to £4 million through his agents in Constantinople, was at some loggerheads with Churchill who saw the Dardanelles expedition as resulting in a 'spark revolution and peace' situation. Thus he saw peace emerging through revolution in Turkey. Had Hall's plan gone through, frustrated as it was by Fisher, no lives would have been wasted and Churchill would not have been forced to resign.

Gazetteer

FIELD MARSHAL HORATIO KITCHENER, 1st Earl (1850–1916). Born in Ireland he was the legendary 'recruiter': 'Your Country Needs You'. He won the Battle of Omdurman and played a key role in the Boer War including the now disgraced concentration camp system. His relations with Churchill were difficult. Churchill shared, with Queen Victoria, abhorrence of Kitchener for his desecration of the Mahdi's tomb and particularly of his order that all wounded Sudanese should be killed after the Battle of Omburman. To all this, Churchill had been an eyewitness. Prior to this, Churchill had been shocked

---

5   An even larger figure of casualties in Germany and Austria after the Armistice
     has been quoted but is disputed by several historians.

by British brutalities in the Parthan Uprising of 1897. Kitchener was drowned on his way to Russia when his ship, the *Hampshire*, struck a mine west of the Orkney Islands. Various conspiracy theories surround the sinking including Russian communists and Irish Republican agents. (p. 53)

RT HON REGINALD MCKENNA (1863–1943). Banker and Liberal politician, he was Asquith's Home Secretary and Chancellor of the Exchequer. He oversaw the War Loans in 1915. When he retired he refused the offer of a peerage. McKenna, as an individual, was not particularly attractive. When the 45-year-old McKenna married Pamela Jekyll, a pretty 19-year-old, her friend Violet Asquith considered him repulsive with his 'spots, spats, spectacles and tricolour tights'. When Churchill was given the Admiralty McKenna was devastated as he had long coveted the position. His resentment lingered on and when war was declared in 1914 he was playing golf while criticising Churchill as someone who 'has never done anything big'. (p. 52)

WALTER RUNCIMAN, 1st Viscount of Doxford (1870–1949). Son of a shipping magnate, in 1914 he was President of the Board of Trade under Asquith until the government fell in 1916. Later, in 1938, he was sent to Munich by Chamberlain and his report, regrettably, endorsed the return of the Sudetenland to Germany. (p. 56)

Chapter 5: The Cruise of the *Sayonara*

Hall notes 'To be shown to Comdr Simon, C. Serocold, Officer from *Cornwallis*, Sir Arthur Shirley Benn'. Later Hall writes that Simon had vetted the text and that Lord Sligo's name would not be given unless Sligo approved. All official dispatches had been seen at the Admiralty.

The SY *Sayonara* was about 600 tons and flew the Stars and Stripes. The owner was a Colonel McBride, but 'he looked like a Hun'. McBride: citizen of the USA? Actually, Major William Russell Howell, CBE, DSO (1865–1930), an extraordinary British Army officer in 'Darkest Africa', explorer and adventurer. His father had been created a Privy Chamberlain of the Sword and Cape to his Holiness Pope Pius X. Major Howell was originally an engineer in South America and on the Great Western Railway and he was granted leave of absence from the Glamorgan Volunteer Artillery and proceeded to Sierra Leone to develop the railways there. On encountering rebellion he proceeded to take action and virtually single-handedly put down the rebels. (See *The Tablet*, 19 April 1930.)

More than twenty-five personalities are noted, starting with the mythical owner and captain of the yacht.

This highly entertaining tale delivers some important lessons on planned deception. It is a tale of subterfuge of the kind for which Hall proved himself to be a past master. When Lord Sligo stormed into the Admiralty and berated Hall over the lack of awareness and action against this yacht, 'planting mines in Westport Harbour', Hall was forced to divulge some of the truth: the 'owner' was a Major in the British Army and the 'American' captain, or 'skipper', was a naval lieutenant, Lieutenant F.M. Simon RNR, 'who served with me in the *Queen Mary*'. Simon was an unusual man. He had sailed as a navigator in the airship *America II*, the first airship to cross the Atlantic. He was the only Englishman in the crew. Later he served with the Cunard Line and, on the lower deck, was invariably called 'the Yank'.

HMS *Queen Mary* was the last battlecruiser of the Royal Navy. She fought at Heligoland Bight, missed the Battle of Dogger Bank as she was refitting but fought at Jutland. Hit by the *Derfflinger* her magazines exploded with the loss of 1,226 officers and men. Only twenty survived.

Casement's own story (1864–1916) is that of an Irish patriot and British consular official. He condemned the treatment of native workers in the Congo and in Peru. He organised the Anti-Slavery Society. He then joined the Irish Volunteers in 1915 and sought German help for Irish independence. Arrested and condemned to death for high treason he was hanged in Pentonville

Prison at the age of 51. Half a million people filled past his coffin in Glasnevin Cemetery in Dublin.

The Anglo-Irish Lord Sligo was actually Colonel Arthur Howe Brown (1867–1951) 8th Marquis of Sligo, KBE. An Irish soldier in the Royal Munster Fusiliers, 'he believed in God, the British Empire and Westport in that order'. His coffin was draped in the Union Jack by the local, respected undertaker who had been a general in the Old IRA.

Hall notes that later developments showed that the *Sayonara* 'had not sailed in vain'. His story ends with the attempt to entrap Sir Roger Casement, an attempt which was frustrated by his sudden and unexpected return to Germany. Thus, the artificial presentation of a 'foreign' ship could, and did, put at the disposal of the Intelligence Services a mechanism whereby the enemy might be trapped. What examples may have followed that manoeuvre in the Second World War and later?

Gazetteer

SIR ARTHUR SHIRLEY BENN (1858–1937), MP for Plymouth South, politician and business man. Was made 1st Baron Glenravel of Kensington. (p. 69)

JOHANN HEINRICH VON BERNSTORFF (1862–1939), son of a powerful Prussian politician, he became a member of the Reichstag. He married Jeanne Luckemeyer, a wealthy New York German-Austrian. From 1908 till 1917 he was German Ambassador to the US and Mexico. In 1914 he was recruited into German Intelligence and provided with an immense slush fund which he used to finance the sabotage of American installations, the Welland Canal near Niagra Falls and the Canadian Railways. The Black Tom explosion in Jersey City, New Jersey, USA, in 1916 was largely his work. Damage was estimated at $20 million plus damage to the Statue of Liberty at $100,000. Seventy people died and hundreds were injured. His philandering and other activities were exposed by British Intelligence. He supported the Indian movement for independence.

Later he supported the founding of the Jewish State in Palestine and was criticised by Hitler as one of those bearing 'the guilt and responsibility for the collapse of Germany'. On the Nazis being elected to power he left Germany for Switzerland where he died. (p. 68; his Countess is on p. 152)

CAPTAIN KARL BOY-ED (1872–1930), German naval attaché to Bernstorff. Multi-talented and widely travelled he was involved in sabotage and spying in America. He suffered from a rare disease, phagomania, and insomnia and died of a riding accident on his 58th birthday. (p. 69)

ADLER CHRISTENSEN (1890–??), Casement's Norwegian bodyguard and manservant. Suspected to have been a double agent, he was offered £5,000 and immunity from the law (in writing by the British Ambassador to Ireland, Manfield Finlay) if he would betray his employer. According to the *Republican News*, January 2002, he did not do so. Other versions claim he did. (p. 77)

CAPTAIN, 'a wealthy Yankee', actually LT F.M. SIMON RNR who had served with 'Blinker' in HMS *Queen Mary*. Later, a commander. (p. 71)

ADMIRAL SIR CHARLES COKE, Naval Commander of the West Coasts of Ireland (1854–1945), became a vice admiral in 1913 having been ADC to the King in 1907. (p. 59)

DANIEL F. COHALAN (1867–1946), New York lawyer, politician and judge. Involved in many Irish–American societies perhaps including the Irish *Clan na Gael* group possibly linked to with the Black Tom explosion. He helped plan and finance the Easter Rising and the sending of Casement to Germany. (p. 68)

HMS *CORNWALLIS*. Commissioned 1904 and based on Portland. She moved to the Mediterranean and later Gallipoli. Torpedoed in the Med she remained afloat long enough to save 705 out of her complement of 720. (p. 60)

JOHN DEVOY (1842–1928), Irish rebel leader who helped to fund the Irish Volunteers. Worked closely with Bernstorff, Casement and Cohalan. (p. 69)

MR ANTHONY DREXEL (1874–1948). Full name: Anthony Joseph Drexel Biddle, Sr. Scion of the wealthy Drexel Bank, the son of 'The Man Who Made Wall Street' and groomed Pierpont Morgan. His origins were Austrian. An eccentric multi-millionaire, he served in the Marines, was a boxer and wrote for sporting papers in America. An active Christian, he founded 'Athletic Christianity' which counted 300,000 members around the world. (p. 70)

MR R.J. HANNON, 'energetic' secretary of the Navy League, a pressure group to get the Royal Navy up to date. His initiation of its Aerial Defence Committee resulted in the Navy League being asked to take over the National Aeronautical Defence Association. (p. 70)

KARL HANS LODY (1877–1914). AKA Charles A. Juglis Inglis. Spied on Royal Navy ships in Scotland resulting in the sinking of HMS *Pathfinder*, the first ship ever sunk by a torpedo fired by a submarine. Fled to Ireland but was captured by Thomson's Irish operatives, tried and executed as a spy in the Tower of London. (p. 68)

CAPTAIN F. LE MESURIER was captain of the battleship HMS *Cornwallis*. (p. 60)

MJÖLNIR. 600-ton Danish steamer from Oslo supposed to be carrying Casement but his voyage had been postponed. The name is a Viking one, meaning 'That Which Smashes'. (p. 77)

NAVY LEAGUE. It was founded in 1894 to promote public awareness of the importance of British sea power. By 1914 it had 100,000 members. By 1976 it had become responsible only for Sea Cadets and the Girl's Nautical Training Corps and was renamed the Sea Cadet Association. (p. 64)

MR ALMERIC PAGET, 1st Baron Queenborough (1861–1949), grandson of Wellington's cavalry commander at Waterloo. Worked first for the Midland Railway, emigrated to the USA, became a cowboy and a real estate agent, self-made industrialist and award-winning yachtsman. Elected to Parliament in Westminster. Founded the Almeric Paget Massage Corps in 1914 which treated 200 soldiers a day. After the war it provided free care for the poor of London. Multitudinous responsibilities followed and he became fiercely opposed to Bolshevism and was a supporter of Franco and Hitler, even as late as 1939. (p. 70)

FRANZ VON PAPEN ZU KÖNINGEN (1879–1969), wealthy Catholic nobleman on the German General Staff in 1913 and was then military attaché to the USA. His sabotage activities and espionage in the USA were extensive resulting in his expulsion in 1916. Fleeing a federal grand jury he then served on the Western Front, became a Major in the Ottoman Army and was involved in the supply of arms to the Irish for the Easter Rising. He also conspired with the Hindu Nationalists in India. In 1932 he became Chancellor of Germany and served as Vice Chancellor under Hitler in 1933–34. His chequered and contradictory career continued and he was only saved from death in the Night of the Long Knives by Göring's 'protective custody'. Arrested in 1945 by 1st Lieutenant Thomas McKinley of the 194th Glider Infantry, he was acquitted at the Nuremberg War Crimes Trial but was subsequently sentenced to eight years hard labour at the age of 65 by a West German denazification court. He was released on appeal. He died aged 89. (p. 69)

HMS *RUSSELL*. Pre-Dreadnought battleship, commissioned 1903, served in the 6th Battle Squadron and covered the BEF movement to France. Assisted with the Dardanelles evacuation, she struck two sea mines (laid by submarine *U-73*), was set on fire and sank off Malta. (p. 71)

HMS *SAFEGUARD*. Patrol and examination vessel ex-Coastguard and Fishing Protection. 875 tonnes, 2 x 3pdr guns. Based in Queenstown, 1914–1918.

Other sources referred to her as a 'DAMS' (Defensibly Armed Merchant Ship). DAMS resulted from the strengthening of selected ships during construction to allow for the rapid fitting of armaments. The exact description of the *Safeguard* is uncertain. (p. 59)

SINN FÉIN. Irish Republican Party founded 1909. The name means 'We Ourselves'. Associated with the Irish Volunteers and an active participant in the Easter Rising in 1916. With de Valera's resignation it lost the financial support of the USA and the Party dwindled. Its main goal is a United Ireland. (p. 64)

SIR BASIL THOMSON, 1861–1939. Colonial administrator, prison governor, police and intelligence officer. Worked closely with 'Blinker' Hall. Used double-agents in Ireland, such as J.C. Bymes, who identified Michael Collins, but was caught and executed by the IRA. Director of Intelligence in 1919 with overall charge of all intelligence in Great Britain but resigned in 1921. (p. 69)

WAR SIGNAL STATION (W. SS). A site guarding the approaches where shipping can be identified and from which signals can be made to ships at sea. Largely developed about 1825 but the concept goes back some 900 years. (p. 60)

Chapter 6: A Little 'Information' for the Enemy

The Battle of Jutland, the greatest sea battle of the war, was fought 31 May to 1 June 1916. Hall remarks that it was not generally known that after the Battle of Jutland on 19 August 1916 the whole of the Grand Fleet put to sea again. This putting to sea of the Grand Fleet was a subterfuge by Hall in collaboration with Admiral Beatty.

Jellicoe and Beatty hardly need summarising but their records are well worth mentioning here. John Rushworth Jellicoe, 1st Earl (1859–1935), was a great moderniser of the Royal Navy developing the Dreadnoughts and submarines. He fought the battles of Heligoland Bight, Dogger Bank and Jutland. Jellicoe was described by Churchill as the only man who could lose the war in an afternoon. Jellicoe knew this. Disagreeing with the policies of Sir Eric Geddes he was unjustly dismissed as a 'defeatist' and was made Governor of New Zealand. The failure of Naval Intelligence at Jutland, later attributed to Admiral Sir Thomas Jackson, is well described in Ramsay's *Spymaster*. In Hall's autobiography there is one incomplete note on Jutland and Ralph Straus 'lost' his correspondence with Beatty on this issue. Here we may see the concern of the Admiralty to screen Hall's criticisms of certain individuals, namely Jackson.

Admiral Lord David Beatty, 1st Earl (1871–1936), participated in the China War of 1900. He destroyed three German cruisers at Heligoland Bight, sank the *Blücher* at Dogger Bank. At Jutland, the hardest fought Royal Navy battle of the war, Beatty commanded the 1st Battlecruiser Squadron. His aggressive approach contrasted with the caution of Jellicoe. He is remembered for his comment at the battle, 'There seems to be something wrong with our bloody ships today.' Beatty became First Sea Lord in 1919.

Returning to Hall's stratagem his fifth point, which he qualifies as 'offensive' work, that is information deliberately given to the enemy, is in contrast to the four chief points he previously noted as being of significance in intelligence work. The four 'defensive' points were Spy Systems and Agents; Economic and Blockage information through Insurance; Neutral Countries; and Wireless and Cypher Interception.

In his fifth point the Germans were passed 'secret information' in order to establish with them the authenticity of their informant and so provide a channel back from Germany of the information that Room 40 was seeking.

Hall refers to Lt Col Drake, DSO (1876–1943), of the Counter-Espionage Service. The fruitfulness of full co-operation between the naval and military departments in this type of deception is significant. Drake had been in the North Staffordshire Regiment in the Boer War and then entered the CIS. He was Assistant to Vernon Kell, founder of MI5. Associated with Cumming's work with double agents in Holland and Germany he was highly decorated by the Allied countries.

The substitution and alteration of the photograph of the *Petropavlovsk* to resemble the *Lion* is an early example of this process of disinformation which is so familiar to us in the media today. The *Petropavlovsk* had been launched in 1894 at a cost of £1,098,000. Sunk in the Russo-Japanese war after an attempt to attack the *Asagiri* and *Hayutori*: 700 perished and 88 were saved. The Grand Duke Cyril was slightly wounded. The *Lion* was a 26,270-ton battlecruiser of 1910, built to combat the German Moltke-class battlecruisers which were more powerful than the Royal Navy equivalents. Badly damaged at the Dogger Bank and again at Jutland she was under repair for many months. She completed her war service on North Sea patrols and was sold for scrap in 1924.

Hall also refers to Colonel Nicolai (1873–1947) the first senior intelligence officer of the Imperial German Army who ran *Abteilung IIIb*, the military secret service. Although retired, by the end of the Second World War he was arrested by the Soviet NKVD, interrogated in Moscow and died in custody in the Butyrka Prison, cremated and buried in a mass grave in the Donskoy Monastery. In 1999 he was formally exonerated of all charges by the Russian military prosecutors.

Claude Serocold (1875–1959) was a successful Old Etonian stockbroker and was Personal Assistant to 'Blinker' Hall. He was recommended by Hall to any future DNI.

In the case of the Socialist Women's Conference in Berne in March 1915, the three-line sentence referring to his 'unhappy twenty four-hours' is marked for deletion. The notable women listed here are Clara Zetkin, Miss Margaret Bondfield, Miss Jane Adams and Mrs Pankhurst and her daughter Christabel. So outstanding were these ladies they are described here in detail.

Clara Zetkin (1857–1933) was a German Marxist theorist and organiser of the first International Women's Day. She was a co-founder of the Spartacist League and sat in the Reichstag 1920–33, going into exile in the USSR on the rise of Hitler. She was buried in Red Square. Another woman connected with this affair was Miss Margaret Grace Bondfield (1873–1953). She was a Labour politician and the first woman to become a Cabinet minister as Minister of Labour, appointed by Ramsay MacDonald.

Thirdly there was Miss Jane Adams (1866–1935). She was born in Cedarville, Illinois and was a pioneer leader in women's suffrage, social work and world peace. Her father founded the Republican Party and was a friend of Abraham Lincoln. Contracting Pott's disease in early life she suffered lifelong health problems. Her work for women, children and social ethics was extensive and influential. In 1915 she was President of the Women's International League for Peace and Freedom. She was awarded the Nobel Peace Prize in 1931.

In 1903 Emmeline Pankhurst (1857–1928) founded the Women's Social & Political Union and campaigned for women's suffrage. She lived an itinerant lifestyle, was imprisoned, force-fed and often targeted by the police. On war breaking out her movement abandoned all militant activities until the war was over. Her energy and determination for the patriotic advocacy for the war was the same as for women's suffrage. She joined the Conservative Party in 1926 but she died from exhaustion occasioned by her sufferings two years later, aged 69. She was 'the supreme protagonist for the electoral enfranchisement of women', *New York Herald Tribune*. Her daughter Christabel joined her at speaking events and her four other children all became involved.

Reference is made to the SS *Kronprinz Wilhelm* which was, for the ID, 'a complete failure'. This remarkable ship was a world breaking German passenger boat and she became a very successful commerce raider. Having sunk some 50,000 tons of Allied shipping she was forced to put into port as her crew were suffering from scurvy. She was turned into a troopship by the US Navy and was finally scrapped in 1923.

Gazetteer

WALTER CUNLIFFE (1855–1920), merchant banker and Governor of the Bank of England. His grandfather had developed the North Eastern Railway. The Cunliffe Committee oversaw the restoration of Britain's economy in 1918. (p. 95)

THE BATTLE OF THE FALKLANDS is said to have been generated through several different scenarios. In one of these Room 40 is said to have sent a false signal which lured von Spee's squadron onto the guns of the waiting British battlecruiser squadron. Some authorities doubt this because such a message might have told the Germans that their code had been broken. Room 40, it is said, would have used broken codes defensibly and not offensively. Churchill himself took the issue up with Jellicoe, emphasising the vital importance of keeping the Germans in the dark regarding their broken codes. It was Franz von Rintelen, the 'Dark Invader', who is said to have made other suggestions concerning code interceptions to Hall, but his testimony here, as in other cases, is not regarded as being reliable. Von Rintelen became a personal friend of Hall's and was largely persona grata in Great Britain, to which he moved in 1920. He died in England in 1949. (p. 99)

SIR JOHN FRENCH, 1st Earl of Ypres (1852–1925). Anglo-Irish Field Marshal, became first commander-in-chief of the BEF, 1914–1915. A complex and contradictory character, his womanising was unequalled. His role during in the First World War ('war on a gigantic scale') and later in Ireland is unquestionable. (p. 91)

GOULD is the alias for Schroeder who owned a pub in Rochester. (p. 82)

ARMGAARD KARL GRAVES (1882–19??). Arrested in Glasgow and put on trial in Edinburgh as an alleged spy, 22 July 1912. He possessed a German telegraphic code giving particulars of guns under construction at Beardmores Works, maps of the Firth of Forth, along with poisons and hypodermic materials. (p. 82) This same Graves, who self-styled himself as an 'international spy', later attempted to blackmail Countess von Bernstorff. He claimed that the countess and her friends had made $1 million on receiving advance knowledge of the activities of U-53. (Chapter 25; p. 152)

THOMAS MARLOWE, editor of the *Daily Mail* from 1899. (p. 67) Mr H.W. Wilson was a staff writer on the *Daily Mail* who collaborated with Hall on deception disinformation. (p. 95)

RALPH NEVILLE, possibly a descendent of Ralph Neville, 1st Earl of Westmorland, Raby Castle, Durham (1364–1425). 'Indiscreet' agent of Hall's by which he passed on 'secret' information to his fellow club members, some of whom were working for Germany. Thus they were hoist by their own petard. (p. 93)

LORD NORTHCLIFFE, later Lord Harmsworth (1865–1922). Pioneer of mass circulation newspapers, born in Dublin. He took over *The Times* in 1914 and campaigned against Lloyd George and Lord Kitchener but later he directed a war mission in the USA and in 1918 became responsible for British propaganda. (p. 94)

GUNNER PARROTT, No. 119045, Royal Garrison Artillery, who worked on manned coastal batteries, mounted and siege guns. These were employed on the Somme and at Arras, in Gibraltar and Bermuda. (p. 82)

PETROPAVLOVSK. Launched 1894, she cost over £1 million. Sunk in the Russo-Japanese war in 1904 on returning to Port Arthur after an attempt to attack the Japanese Navy – 700 perished and eighty-eight were saved including Grand Duke Cyril. (p. 86)

REINHARD VON SCHEER (1863–1928) was the Admiral controlling the High Seas Fleet at the Battle of Jutland. He instituted unrestricted submarine warfare, 'the only option to defeat Great Britain'. In 1918 the German fleet mutinied and all naval action was abandoned. (p. 80)

SIR EUSTACE TENNYSON D'EYNCOURT, 1st Baronet, FRS (1868–1951). Brilliant naval architect and engineer of some of the most famous British battleships. In 1915 Churchill made him responsible for the first military tanks to be used in warfare. (p. 86)

BATTLE OF TSUSHIMA, a major engagement of Russo-Japanese War, May 1905. Two-thirds of the Russian fleet were destroyed after a voyage of 18,000 miles. A peace treaty was signed in September 1905. It was the first naval battle in which wireless telegraphy played an important role, the Japanese using their own material, the Russians relying on German manufactures which they found difficult to use and maintain. (p. 86)

Chapter 7: Lord Fisher and Mr Churchill

Hall noted that this chapter was to be seen by Lord Reading, Capt. Grease, Griffin Eady and George Lambert.

Lord Reading was Rufus Daniel Isaacs, 1st Marquis of Reading (1860–1935). Great advocate and solicitor-general, later attorney-general. Lord Chief Justice in 1913 and, during the war, special envoy to the USA negotiating financial plans. Afterwards, Chairman of United Newspapers and of ICI.

Captain Grease was Naval Assistant to Fisher and was associated with Geddes, 1st Lord of the Admiralty in 1917. He played an important role in trying to get Fisher back to the Admiralty.

Griffin Eady had a deep knowledge of Turkey and was contacted by Hall to establish liaison with Gerald Fitzmaurice in Constantinople. This was to set up an intelligence network in the Near East. Griffin Eady was head of Sir John Jackson Ltd, important contractors.

George Washington Lambert (1873–1930) was an Australian First World War war artist who covered the ANZAC landing at Gallipoli in 1915.

The chapter begins with the return of Lord Fisher to the Admiralty only three weeks after Hall's appointment in Whitehall. Hall notes that Fisher and his own father had known each other for years. Hall evidences the greatest respect for Fisher, as does the navy as a whole. Fisher had asked 'Blinker' to be his commander in the *Inflexible*. This ship played a significant role in Room 40's work in that she chased the *Goeben* and the *Breslau* in the Med and, later, with the *Invincible* sank the *Scharnhorst* (from which there were no survivors) and the *Gneisenau* (from whom 176 survivors were rescued) in the Battle of the Falklands. The British battlecruisers only lost one man killed and five wounded.

The *Inflexible* later bombarded the Turkish forts in the Dardanelles, was damaged by enemy fire and struck a mine. Beached to prevent her sinking she was repaired in Malta and then at Gib. At Jutland she damaged the German battlecruiser *Lützow* and witnessed the destruction of HMS *Invincible*.

Fisher had originally proposed 'Blinker' as Inspecting Captain of the Mechanical Training Establishment in which capacity Hall performed well. Although Fisher's appointment came too late to avert the disaster of Coronel (off the coast of Chile in November 1914) his successful dispatch of battlecruisers to the Falklands reinvigorated the navy, and led to Hall's hope that Fisher would prevail over Churchill, his own personal liking for Churchill notwithstanding.

Then came the matter of the 200 to 300 'submarines' to Zeebrugge. Hall knew that the agent supplying this information always referred to things in or under the water as 'submarines'. Churchill was unaware of this nomenclature and Hall saw no reason for explanations as, normally, such detail would not be pursued by the First Lord.

Later Hall describes the Dardanelles expedition and Lord Fisher's orders for Hall to 'Buy up all the lighters and tugs to be found in Greek waters'. This affair introduced him to Richard Grech. Then a note arrived (via Capt. Grease, Naval Secretary) to find the location of Fitzmaurice, 'possibly in Sophia'. This note also brought in Lord Grey and 'the Bulgarians'. Richard Grech was a ship owner, renting tugs on the River Hoogly, at Gallipoli and in London. His *Dalhouise* was the largest tug of its time and was requisitioned by the Admiralty to augment the ships of Royal Fleet Auxiliary (RFA), but was torpedoed and sunk in April 1918. He bought the RFA *Hughli* in 1907 but in 1915 she was subject to a claim by his brother William. She struck a mine off the Belgian coast in April 1918. With his wide-ranging experience he was the right man to buy up sea craft in Greek waters.

'The earliest wireless message of the war' to be decrypted (German Admiralty Staff, Berlin to *Goeben* via Nauen) is featured in which a proposed alliance with Turkey is put forward with instructions for *Goeben* and *Breslau* to go directly to Constantinople, with the resultant catastrophic consequences.

The German Emperor's telegram of March 1915, addressed to Admiral von Usedom (1854–1925), is reproduced. Von Usedom was a Pomeranian noble who had led the German Expeditionary Force during the Boxer rebellion. In 1914 he developed minefields and established artillery on the Dardanelles resulting in the sinking of the *Irrestible* and *Ocean* of the Royal Navy and the French battleship *Bouvet*. He remained in Turkey to the end of the war.

From the German Emperor's telegram arose the dramatic, and resultant calamitous decision by Fisher (finally endorsed by Churchill) to force the Dardanelles. 'A pretty large sum of money' is referred to in a letter from Hall's 93 Cadogan Gardens address. Had Hall's plan for the seduction of the Turks gone through many lives would have been saved. The £3 million, Hall had promised the Turks, with no authority from anyone, caused a monumental uproar with Churchill and Fisher but Hall's reasoning finally won the day. Fisher demanded the cancellation of Hall's financial offer to the Turks, but he maintained an offer of £200,000 for the *Goeben* and £100,000 for the *Breslau*.

The lesson, that of protecting the Sea Lords from the 'minutiae' of secret intelligence, enabled Hall to pursue a strategy which, successful or not, could not involve the fall of either Churchill or Fisher. By this time Fisher's erratic behaviour and strange language was clearly indicative of some acute form of instability and he had become a worry to those working with him. As an example we can cite Fisher writing to 'his friend' von Tirpitz in Germany in 1916 enthusiastically endorsing Tirpitz' unrestricted submarine warfare policy. 'I'd have done the same myself,' Fisher wrote to 'Dear old Tips'.

As a footnote to this it has to be said that Churchill had gone off his Dardanelles idea and had proposed an attack on the German island of Borkum.

Capture of Borkum would, Churchill argued, be intolerable to the Germans and would probably result in the decisive sea battle envisaged for the North Sea. Fisher and Kitchener fought this idea and finally won him over.

There follows a sympathetic treatment of the Fisher problem, ending with his resignation. Sir Frederick Hamilton's request to Hall to play a major role in the 'resignation' of Fisher is described leading to the denouement of the affair by Rufus Isaacs, Lord Reading. Fisher's appointment to the Board of Inventions was to be his recompense.

News of a gold shipment from Lagos and the danger posed by the *Kronprinz* brought Hall's use of disinformation to the fore in *The Times* which not only fooled the Germans but also the Governor of the Bank of England, Lord Cunliffe.

This chapter serves as a reminder of four factors. One: things are not what they may seem to be; two: 'no one can be fully in possession of all the facts'; three: the role of intelligence individuals in political matters; four: disinformation in the service of the nation. Underpinning factors one and three particularly is the need for the highest possible integrity on the part of the SIS.

Ralph Straus wrote to Hall in 1933 saying that the Admiralty objected to this chapter as it included an account of Fisher's machinations.

Gazetteer

ARTHUR JAMES BALFOUR, 1st Earl (1848–1930), Scottish statesman and philosopher. He followed Churchill as First Lord of the Admiralty and became Foreign Secretary under Lloyd George, 1916–1919. He was responsible for the Balfour Declaration (1917) promising the Zionists a permanent home in Palestine. (p. 114)

BRESLAU. German cruiser transferred to the Ottoman Empire in 1914 and renamed *Midilli*. In company with the *Goeben* she bombarded the Russian coast, transported troops and laid minefields but was damaged by Russian firepower. She was finally sunk in 1918 at the Battle of Imbros with the loss of the vast majority of her 354 officers and crew. (p. 103)

IN THE BATTLE OF CORONEL off the coast of Chile on 1 November 1914, von Spee met and defeated a Royal Navy squadron commanded by Rear Admiral Sir Christopher Craddock. Neither Admiral had expected to meet. The superior German force sank two battleships and Craddock died in the battle along with 1,600 of his men. This was the first battle of the war and the Royal Navy had not lost a battle since the Battle of Lake Champlain in 1812. This led to the Battle of the Falklands where von Spee's force was destroyed and von Spee was killed along with most of his men. (p. 99)

COZENS-HARDY. Member of Room 40, he found the Wassmuss Papers in the India Office on the orders of Hall. (p. 104)

DEDEAGACH, now named Alexandroupoli, is on the Greek mainland opposite Samothrace. The Constantinople Agreement of 1915 was a set of secret assurances that were made by the Triple Alliance which promised Constantinople to the Russians in the event of victory. This was done largely to keep Russia in the war. (p. 103)

ENVER PASHA (1881–1922), leader of the Young Turk Revolution of 1908, he became the main leader of the Ottoman Empire in the Balkan wars and in the First World War. With Talaat and Djemal he was one of the principal perpetrators of the Armenian Genocide. According to one report, he was killed in a Red Army cavalry charge following a surprise attack at his HQ near Dushanbe. The Young Turks were seen by the Arabs as godless transgressors of the Muslim creed, traitors to the highest interests of Islam. (p. 105)

GERALD FITZMAURICE (1865–1939), Chief Dragoman of the British Embassy in Turkey. 'Nothing happens in that city of intrigue without his knowing every detail.' Hall made him into a member of the Naval Intelligence Division. (p. 102)

SIR ERIC CAMPBELL GEDDES (1875–1937), one of Lloyd George's 'men of push and go'. Unfortunately he was made 1st Lord of the Admiralty (1915–1919) and his total ignorance of naval matters, equalled only by Lloyd George's, led to the navy suffering greatly from German submarine warfare. He espoused heavy reparations by Germany at the Versailles Peace Conference which largely contributed, it is said, to the rise of Hitler. (p. 116)

GOEBEN. A German battleship, in 1912 she and the light cruiser *Breslau* patrolled the Mediterranean and in 1914 evaded British naval forces and reached Constantinople. She was renamed the *Yavuz Sultan Selim* in the Ottoman Navy and, with its German crew wearing fezzes, bombarded Russian towns and facilities in the Black Sea thus dragging Turkey into the war on the side of Germany. (p. 103)

GRAND RABBI HAKHAM BASHI, was the overall head of the Jews in the Ottoman Empire. In 1915 it was Hain Nanhum Effendi (1908–1920). He was an Anglophile. (p. 105)

SIR EDWARD GREY OF FALLODON, 1st Viscount (1862–1933), statesman, Liberal MP for Berwick-upon-Tweed. Secretary of State for Foreign Affairs, he negotiated peace in the Balkans and in 1913 distinguished himself in his strives for peace in Europe. 'The lamps are going out all over Europe. We will not see them lit again in our lifetime.' (13 August 1914) Renowned for his writings on birds and fly-fishing but after much family sadness he was totally blind at the end of his life. His blindness is said to have been due to overwork in the dimly lit Home Office. (p. 103)

SIR FREDERICK HAMILTON, 1st Sea Lord. Said to be 'a rather lazy officer of no great distinction', although Hall liked him. It was Hamilton who gave Hall the unpleasant task of removing Fisher. (p. 110)

KAISER WILHELM II (1859–1941), 'The Highest'. Last German Emperor and King of Prussia from 1888 to 1918, he was the eldest grandson of Queen Victoria. He dismissed Bismarck and launched Germany on the road to the First World War. He lost support of the army, abdicated in November 1918 and fled to exile in the Netherlands. In spite of his later support for Hitler, Hitler ordered the dismissal of the German soldiers guarding his house at Doorn where he died of pulmonary embolism. (p. 106)

KUEPFERLE. In 1915 Mabel Elliott uncovered a German spy plot. By chance a letter was found by her in the Royal Society of Chemistry Archives. Fluent in German and Dutch, she worked as a censor in the First World War, and found a letter going to Holland, written in invisible ink. This gave military movements and details of Royal Navy ships around the coast and the forces defending London. Anton Kuepferle, 27 years old, was arrested and, before the conclusion of his trial in the Tower of London, found hanged in his cell. He left a message saying he was a German officer having previously claimed he was an American salesman. (p. 112)

GEORG ALEXANDER VON MÜLLER (1854–1940). Admiral of the German Imperial Navy and close to the Kaiser, he advocated his abdication in 1917 believing the Kaiser to have become a virtual recluse. He agreed to the instigation of unrestricted submarine warfare. (p. 106)

SIR CHARLES ALGERNON PARSONS, FRS (1854–1931), Anglo-Irish inventor of the steam turbine. He had a great influence on naval and engineering developments including optical equipment for searchlights and telescopes. The Dreadnoughts were the fastest battleships in the world due to Parsons' steam turbines. His company is now merged with Siemens, known as Siemens Parsons. (p. 115)

Q-SHIPS. Heavily armed merchant ships used to lure submarines to make surface attacks. So named because Queenstown in Ireland was their homeport. HMS *Saxifrage*, renamed HMS *President*, is a living example on Kings Reach on the Thames. Q-ships were responsible for sinking 10 per cent of all German U-boats destroyed. (p. 96)

SIR JOSEPH JOHN THOMSON, FRS (1856–1940). Nobel Prize winner, great English physicist who discovered the electron and the first subatomic particle. He made many inventions including the mass spectrometer and discovered the 'delta ray'. One of the four board members of the Board of Inventions, he developed anti-submarine devices and much else for the Admiralty. He was also a moral philosopher. (p. 115)

EDWIN WHITTALL OF MODA, Istanbul, CBE (1864–1953). Director of J.W. Whittall and in close contact with the upper echelons of Turkish officialdom and Enver Pasha. Endeavoured to keep Turkey out of the war. Enver Pasha appropriated his house in 1914 and partially destroyed his six Aubusson tapestries. (p. 104)

SIR ARTHUR KYNET WILSON, VC (1842–1921). Became First Sea Lord in 1910, a post offered to him to succeed Fisher. He was 'abusive, inarticulate and autocratic'. Recalled by Churchill in 1914 to advise on strategy he was an early proponent of submarine warfare and advocated the capture of Heligoland. (p. 110)

GERTRUDE MARGARET LOTHIAN BELL (1868–1926). She deserves mention as 'the uncrowned Queen of Iraq' and the brains behind T.E. Lawrence whom she virtually groomed into his role of Lawrence of Arabia. She was also the 'definer' of Middle East policy for Winston Churchill. A photograph of 22 March 1921 shows her in company with these two men, all of them riding on camels in front of the Sphinx at the time of the Cairo conference. Bell was recruited into BNI by 'Blinker' at the urging of David Hogarth (1812–1927) Commander, RNVR (1915–19), and Director of Room 40's Arab Bureau in Cairo, 1916. Her expertise in Arab affairs earned her the loyalty of the Arab Sheiks and respect of the British officials. (p. 14)

Chapter 25: The Zimmermann Telegram and America's entry into the war

The decryption of the Zimmermann Telegram and Hall's strategy and tactics in revealing it has rightly been hailed as the intelligence coup of all time. Few chapters of Hall's autobiography have been quoted more extensively than on this telegram. Ramsay, Hall's most recent biographer, gives no less than two chapters to it in his *Spymaster*, Chapter XI: 'Arthur Zimmermann sends a telegram' and Chapter XII: 'War comes to America, "Alone I did it"'. In addition Ramsay quotes innumerable other sources: Beesly, Halpen, Gilbert, *The Intimate Papers of Colonel House*, Miller's *Theodore Roosevelt*, and many others. Here we reproduce Hall's own writing in full, something never before made public.

Not surprisingly no other chapter introduces so many actors – saints and sinners, one might say – as does this chapter. The story of the greatest intelligence coup of all time, with the extraordinary result of bringing the United States into the war, must inevitably hold pride of place in Hall's autobiography. It is the longest chapter in the book. The detail which Hall gives hardly calls for an extensive commentary, especially as so many academics, historians and intelligence authorities have done this long before its publication here. Reading of their achievements – both for good and for bad – brings out the dimension of Room 40's work on this vital issue initiated by Zimmermann. It is to be noted that several names who might have been mentioned, are missing, and indeed not only from this chapter. Juan March is one of the most outstanding agents to be omitted. He worked with Colonel Thoroton, chief of BNI in Gibraltar. Others not mentioned include Captain John Harvey RN and Henryano Kerchaer, who was Thoroton's Spanish number two.

Hall writes, '… our first knowledge of this surprising communication was derived from European sources.' The surprising communication referred to became known as the Zimmermann Telegram. Hall writes of 'the staff officer in Berlin', someone who had revealed to and through BNI that the Germans were about to attack Verdun – Operation GERICHT. The indiscretion came from an important German official at a cocktail party.

At Verdun, Joffre had chosen to ignore this report while, at the same time, French Intelligence had suffered a severe setback with the loss of sixty of their heroic agents behind enemy lines. These had been led by Louise de Bettignies, 'the Queen of Spies', a courageous 34-year-old French woman who was credited with saving the lives of more than 1,000 British soldiers. She had set up an extraordinary spy and resistance network, based on Lille in February 1915, under her cover name of Alice Dubois. She then met up with Major Kirke of British Military Intelligence (under Major Aylmer Cameron) in Folkestone. She was given a brief course in 'spying' methods in London. As well as using her information for General Haig, BMI and BNI also passed it on to the French. One of her agents carried no less than 300 messages concealed in her clothing. At that time even the possession of a carrier pigeon was a capital offense. She was ultimately discovered by the Germans in October 1915, sentenced to death and then given hard labour for life. She died as a result of untreated illness in a German hospital in September 1918.

A reliable French estimate is that 420,000 French and German soldiers died at Verdun. Alistair Horne in his 1962 *The Price of Glory* graphically describes the 'blight' hanging over Verdun, which persisted in 1979 when we made our own visit. However, given the mindset at French HQ under Joffre, it seems unlikely that any front-line intelligence coming in would have altered his thinking, if 'thinking' was part of his make-up.

Another possible European source for the leakage of German plans and their decryption is Alexander Szek who was transmitting German codes to Room 40 'in the context of the Zimmermann Telegram'. Exfiltrated from Brussels by Hall, he met his death on the ferry from the Netherlands. One can speculate that, as Szek was carrying the 'the final clues to the German cypher', Hall would have wanted to ensure that the entire history of the sources behind this aspect of the Zimmermann Telegram should remain safely under wraps. No official papers exist on Szek from the day he left the Netherlands for England. His case has been studied by several historians without any definitive solutions.

TR16, identified as Dr Karl Krüger, was a German naval engineer who was involved in passing valuable information on German losses in the Battle of Jutland. A total of sixteen German, or German-based, agents are reported in Allan Judd's *The Quest for C*. TR16 travelled between Bremen, Danzig, Kiel, Rostock, Geestemünde, Emden and Wilhelmshaven for his Jutland report. He sent copies to Alexandria, Rome and Petrograd and, on his own copy, Hall noted '100%': a truly exceptional and 'ideal' man. He died, or was 'presumed dead', at the age of 60 at the start of the Second World War. TR16's 1916 report on German ship and submarine construction was described as 'always accurate, up-to-date and of the greatest possible value'.

Judd also notes agent CX183, in Copenhagen, who refers to a 'German agent D15' from Wilhelmshaven.

Elsewhere, Hall speculates on the route taken by German–Mexican code communications, much of their dispatch being through the 'Swedish Roundabout'. In 2006 Peter Freeman[6] wrote *The Zimmermann Telegram Revisited: A Reconciliation Of The Primary Sources*. In this he dispels some long-standing myths and misapprehensions, which he traces to inaccuracies in accounts by British protagonists in the affair. And, one might add, through Hall's own cover-up of the complete truth.

'The Swedish Roundabout' was a complex communication system used by the Germans in Berlin via neutral countries, designed to prevent British interception.[7] It was a major poser for Hall who could trace some of its network, even leading him to speculate on whether Russia or China might be involved! Various historians have posed several possible routes and it seems that more than one route was used by Germany and that several versions of the telegram were sent. The significance of these maps is that 'the Swedish Roundabout' demonstrates the extent of the complexity existing in Room 40 at that time.

It was de Grey who told Hall on 21 September 1916 that:

---

6   *Cryptologia*, Vol. 130, Issue 2.

7   See Maps 5a and 5b.

It is now abundantly clear that telegrams are passing to Washington not intercepted by us [as postal mail] and not transmitted via Buenos Aires [the Swedish Roundabout]. Neither can the telegrams omitted from our series be fitted into the wireless messages from Sayville or Tuckerton – their number is by no means large enough. I consider it likely they are sent via the State Dept. and the USA embassy and might consequently be interceptable there.[8]

Other sources now confirm this, notably von zur Gathen.

In 2007, Joachim von zur Gathen[9] provides proof that the telegram was transmitted from Berlin to Washington *only* in Code 0075, on US diplomatic lines. He features many original documents, some never reproduced before.

Recently Paul Gannon, in his 2010 *Inside Room 40*, favours a single transmission by the US State Department channel. Prior to this Ben Fenton reported in *The Telegraph* (17 October 2005) that the original Zimmermann Telegram had been discovered in the archives of GCHQ. It had been intercepted by Room 40, as it passed along American owned cables through London. On receiving it the German Ambassador in Washington DC, Johann von Bernstorff, forwarded it to his colleague in Mexico City. Hall ordered his agent there, 'Mr H' (Tom Hohler), to get a copy, which he did. This actual telegram is still held by GCHQ, only a copy being given to TNA. Fenton remarks that 'so many documents surrounding this affair were destroyed on the orders of Admiral Sir Reginald "Blinker" Hall … it was assumed the original typed "decrypt" was gone for ever'.

---

8   This paragraph derives from both Freeman and Ramsay. Freeman's book *The Zimmermann Telegram Revisited* and his unpublished draft article M1.1b on the origins of British Diplomatic Cryptology are the sources for this information and are quoted by Ramsay op. cit.

9   *Cryptologia*, Vol. 31, Issue 2–37.

In 2015 James Wyllie and Michael McKinley's *Codebreakers* was published by Ebury Press. They point out that Hall wanted the von Bernstorff to von Eckardt telegram, as its stamp and serial numbers would be different from the one intercepted by Room 40. This was to be Tom Hohler's work.

Hall included neutral countries such as Switzerland and Spain as being possible parts of the 'Swedish Roundabout'. Gibraltar BNI Station (operating throughout neutral Spain) held one of Hall's most effective networks. Nevertheless, the Berlin agent and Alexander Szek remain as the most probable candidates for being the 'European sources'.

Hall himself described this whole event as 'possibly the biggest thing of the war', a statement endorsed by many historians. It not only brought the USA into the war at a time when increased manpower was essential for the Allies on the Western Front but it also laid the foundation of the UK and USA co-operation which came to fruition on D-Day and the liberation of Europe during the Second World War.

Three lessons at the very least can be drawn from Hall's text: first, the vital importance of never ignoring even trivial information and combining this with exact timing and recognised gamble; second, the interaction of politics in the field of secret intelligence work and, in the case of the telegram, particularly American politics; third, the effectiveness and indeed need of massive disinformation to muddy the waters and to put the enemy off the scent. It can be said that this chapter demonstrates the almost metaphysical nature of intelligence work in that it makes explicit the concept that what is seen is not necessarily the fact. It also raises the intriguing question of national character and culture influencing, even determining, the methods, thinking and usage of secret intelligence. This question of the influence of national culture has been well demonstrated in the *German Analysis of British Secret Service*.[10]

---

10   See Annex E of *Finding Thoroton*.

The galaxy of characters involved runs to over forty and it brings out the dimensions of Room 40's work. Many academics and professional historians have researched the telegram and Hall's account, long before its reproduction here in its totality. The following gazetteer is not only necessarily extensive but it provides a deep insight into the varied factors affecting the individuals involved as well as intelligence decrypting and usage by Room 40.

Gazetteer

EDWARD BELL (1882–1924) was 2nd Secretary of the US Embassy in London. He knew more military secrets than any other American. He met with Hall in February 1917 and was horrified by the Zimmermann Telegram. He is credited with being the 'cement' between Hall, Serocold and Hershell and Ambassador Page and the US Foreign Affairs Department. He died young, aged 42, as a result of a fall in his embassy in Peking. (p. 136)

THEOBOLD VON BETHMANN HOLLWEG (1856–1921) was Chancellor of the German Empire, 1909–1917. He pursued a policy of détente with Britain in order to put a halt to the ruinous arms race; worked with Sir Edward Grey during the Balkan crisis but falsified Grey's letter advocating mediation between the Austrians and Serbs in order to ensure that Austria attacked Serbia. He steered a middle route ending, after the war, offering himself for trial on war crimes. This appeal was rejected by the Allies. (p. 122)

SIR RONALD HUGH CAMPBELL (1883–1953). An outstanding British diplomat, he held several important positions in the Foreign Office and during the Second World War saw further service including as British Ambassador to France at the time France capitulated to Germany in 1940. (p. 137)

VENUSTIANO CARRANZA (1859–1920), President of Mexico in 1917. One of the leaders of the Mexican Revolution. Lukewarm to German overtures to Mexico, his rule was far from free of corruption. He was possibly assassinated but much evidence exists that he shot himself rather than being killed in a surprise night-time attack by forces under General Herrero. (p. 125)

SIR EDWARD HENRY CARSON, Baron (1854–1935). Politician, judge and brilliant advocate at the Bar, famous for his advocacy in the Oscar Wilde and Cadbury Bros cases. Indirectly involved with the Howth gunrunning, he organised the Ulster Volunteers and was violently opposed to Home Rule. 'Ulster will fight and Ulster will be right,' said Lord Randolph Churchill. He is recognised as the founder of today's Northern Ireland. (p. 121)

HERR FOLKE CRONHOLM (1873–1945). Swedish chargé d'affaires in Mexico City, 1913–1916. Advocate of German policies, he sought a German decoration through the offices of Herr von Eckardt, German Minister to Mexico. Dismissed following revelations of his intrigues and secret work for Germany. (p. 122)

JOSÉ DE LA CRUZ PORFIRIO MORI DÍAZ (1830–1915). Mexican soldier and politician, several times President of Mexico, with the rank of general. A controversial figure in Mexican history, he imprisoned his electoral rival and declared himself the winner of an eighth term in office. After his downfall he fled to France where he died in exile four years later. (p. 137)

THE *DEUTSCHLAND* was a German blockade breaker merchant submarine converted into the *U-155*. Her crew were feted in Baltimore in 1916. Amongst her achievements was the transhipment of a $17.5 million cargo of nickel, tin and crude rubber. Later she shipped $10 million worth of gems, securities and medical products and then 6.5 tons of silver bullion. After surrendering in 1918 she was exhibited in the Pool of London. While being broken up for scrap, an explosion ripped the ship apart. (p. 121)

HEINRICH VON ECKARDT (1861–1944). A Baltic German diplomat, he was resident minister in Mexico, 1914–1918. He was opposed to Carranza's government. He pleaded for a decoration for Cronholm, his intercepted message revealing to Hall the nature of Swedish duplicity leading to the decryption of the Zimmermann Telegram. He did not believe the news of the Armistice and his confusion over anticlericalism brought an unsuccessful career to an end. (p. 122)

SIR JAMES ALFRED EWING (1855–1935). Scottish engineer, professor of Engineering at Tokyo (1878), Dundee (1883) and Cambridge (1890). Director of Naval Education, 1916–1929. Known as the Father of Room 40, he managed the cryptanalysis department and oversaw the deciphering of the Zimmermann Telegram. (p. 122)

FREDERICK VIII, a Swedish liner on which the American Secret Service were said to have found the trunk containing the Zimmermann Telegram. (p. 152)

ADMIRAL SIR GUY REGINALD GAUNT (1869–1953), Australian born Royal Navy officer in counter-intelligence. In 1914 he was naval attaché to the US and infiltrated the Hindu-German conspiracy and then headed the Czech Intelligence network. He served also on the Atlantic convoys and was appointed to Naval Intelligence at the Admiralty the same year, 1918. (p. 120)

NIGEL DE GREY (1886–1951). Code-breaker, grandson of the 5th Lord Walsingham. Transferred from service in Belgium (RNVR) to Room 40. With Dilly Knox and William Montgomery he decrypted the Zimmermann Telegram. Promoted to oversee the NID's Mediterranean code-breaking he also liaised with Italian Naval Intelligence and focussed on Austria traffic. During the Second World War he was assigned to Bletchley Park and in 1941 provided Churchill with the first references from German authorities on their atrocities and genocidal activities in occupied territories. As deputy director of GCHQ he worked on Soviet cable traffic. (p. 122)

CHARLES HARDINGE, 1st Baron of Penshurst (1858–1944). British diplomat and statesman who served as Viceroy of India 1910–1916. In 1907 he had declined the post of Ambassador to the US. As Viceroy of India he was an admirer of Ghandi, in spite of assassination attempts by Hindu Nationalists. In 1916 he became Permanent Under-Secretary at the Foreign Office and, in 1920 Ambassador to France. He retired in 1922. (p. 133)

DR WALTER HINES PAGE (1855–1918). Journalist and US Ambassador to the UK during the First World War, and editor of the *Atlantic Monthly*, he played a significant role in bringing the USA into the war and augmented American-British co-operation. Approved the UK blockade and 'black list' programme. A memorial plaque in Westminster Abbey honours his memory. (p. 119)

PAUL VON HINTZE (1864–1941). German naval officer and diplomat. He experienced the tumultuous events in Mexico from 1910 onwards and played a significant role in protecting German citizens in the Civil War. In China from 1914 to 1915, he then served in Norway and was made German Foreign Minister in December 1918 where he participated in the push for an armistice. (p. 124)

TOM HOHLER, Sir Thomas Beaumont Hohler, known as 'H' (1871–1946). British chargé d'affaires in Mexico City in 1916. Original discoverer of the Zimmermann Telegram by obtaining all Cronholm's and von Eckardt's cables. Collaborated with Hall on his autobiography. (p. 124)

KINKEL was involved in the Magnus affair. He claimed that even the most secret telegrams were available to the whole of the embassy staff. He is said to have told Eckardt that the Zimmermann Telegram was 'forwarded from the embassy via Cape Cod' (von Rintelen, *The Dark Invader*). (p. 154)

LACONIA, launched in 1911 she was converted into an armed merchant cruiser in 1914. She patrolled the South Atlantic and the Indian Ocean and was the HQ ship for the attack on German East Africa. Returned to Cunard passenger service in 1916 she was torpedoed by *U-50* off Fastnet with the loss of twelve crew and passengers while returning from the US with seventy-five passengers on board. (p. 143)

ROBERT LANSING (1864–1928), Secretary of State to President Woodrow Wilson from 1915 to 1920. Advocate of the freedom of the seas and the rights of neutral countries, he later advocated American participation in the war on the Allied side. In 1916 he initiated a group of special agents, which became the Bureau of Secret Intelligence and, finally, the US Diplomatic Security Service. (p. 119)

LLOYD-GEORGE OF DWYFOR (1863–1945). Brilliant Welsh Liberal statesman; in 1915 Minister of Munitions; in 1916 War Secretary. Prime Minister in succession to Asquith in 1916. He became an arch-rival of Churchill and later plotted with the appeasement group (the 'Cliveden set') and their associates in royal circles. In 1936 he visited and praised Hitler. (p. 120)

HERR MAGNUS, councillor of the German Legation in Mexico City. Secretary to Eckardt, he became embroiled in Berlin's concern over the leakage of their cable messages. He is described as 'fat' and was stabbed in the stomach, only his excessive flesh covering saving his life. He decrypted the Zimmermann Telegram, which he hid in his bedroom, finally burning the originals. (p. 124)

THE PRESBYTERIAN MINISTER, Rev William Montgomery (1871–??) was a translator of German theological works until he turned code-breaker. With de Grey he completed the decrypt of the Zimmermann Telegram. (p. 144)

GENERAL JOHN 'BLACK JACK' PERSHING (1860–1948). Fought the Apaches and Sioux in the Indian Wars. He participated in the invasion of Mexico in 1916. He led the American Army to France and into combat for the first time at the 2nd Battle of the Marne. His reliance on mass infantry attacks with little artillery support resulted in high casualty rates. He ordered his troops to continue fighting after the signing of the Armistice resulting in 3,500 US casualties, an act regarded as murder by several of his officers. He became an outspoken advocate of aid to Britain during the Second World War. The last four years of his life were spent in a Washington hospital. (p. 125)

THE ROUND TABLE. None of its members have been traced except for Stone. The report emanates from Admiral Guy Reginald Gaunt, Australian-born Royal Navy officer in counter-intelligence. British naval attaché to the US he infiltrated the Hindu-German conspiracy and then headed the Czech Intelligence network. He served on the Atlantic convoys and was appointed to Naval Intelligence at the Admiralty in 1919. He was the guest at the Round Table meeting of 2 March 1917. He convinced the pro-German sceptics, including Stone, that the telegram was genuine. The Round Table had been set up by Lord Milner and Philip Kerr under the direction of Cecil Rhodes who called it the 'Society of the Elect', a secret society. It originated the Royal Society of International Affairs (RSIA) and the Council for Foreign Relations (CFR). (p. 147)

CECIL SPRING RICE (1859–1918), British Ambassador to Sweden and Iran and then to the USA, 1912–18. A poet and an aristocrat, he was an ardent supporter of Roosevelt and best man at his wedding. His untiring efforts to get the US to join the Allies and his frustration of the activities of the German Ambassador in Washington led to the British government publicly recognising his extraordinary contribution to the war effort. (p. 144)

MR STONE was a Democrat Senator for Missouri, described as being 'almost worshipped by his followers' at his memorial service. He was an associate of George Sylvester Viereck, editor of *The Fatherland*, a secret German agent. He declared that the telegram was 'a forgery by the British Secret Service' and was one of the six senators who voted against the US declaration of war against Germany. (p. 147)

GUSTAV BRAUN VON STUMM (1890–1963), German diplomat, involved in the Berlin to Mexico cables affair. He was the initiator of the Baedeker Raids on Britain during the Second World War. (p. 154)

SS *SUSSEX*, a cross-Channel passenger ferry, was torpedoed by a U-boat in 1916. The casualties included several Americans, news of which caused a diplomatic uproar. (p. 131)

EDWARD THURSTAN ('T'), British consul general in Mexico City, briefed by Tom Hohler on the interception of German and Swedish cables. He passed the incriminating telegram to Hall, enabling Hall to state that the it had been obtained in Mexico and decyphered in London. (p. 119)

THE *U-53* sank seventy-nine merchant ships – a total of 213,987 tons of shipping. Her presence in American waters raised anger in American circles. Sir Edward Grey smoothed over the ill feeling concerning the lack of American support for British ships attacked by *U-53*. This sub later operated in the English Channel sinking a further ten ships – a tonnage of 1,782. (p. 121)

PRESIDENT THOMAS WOODROW WILSON (1856–1924). Democrat, elected President in 1916. His remarkable career in academe and politics ended in tragic failure and physical breakdown. He was also the victim of blackmail. His '14 Points' pioneering the League of Nations at the Versailles Peace Conference was opposed by Britain but nonetheless help to lay the foundations of American foreign policy to this day. (p. 121)

AFTERMATH

Reading the full autobiography brings us much closer to Admiral Hall than extracts can which are quoted in respect of specific incidents. One is led to speculation on the character, intelligence and flair of such a man. Where did Hall's undoubted abilities spring from? What role did his childhood, family environment, education and naval career, and indeed his genes, play in forming the man? This is a perennial question facing every individual.

To return from speculative theorising to the text itself we may legitimately ask ourselves what the missing chapters might have included. On the naval front we know that mention of Admiral Jellicoe's and Admiral Beatty's naval battle reforms played a role, as did Sir Thomas Jackson's Jutland error. The decyphering of coded wireless signals was another barrier to publication. Some of the political contents touching on the Cabinet and governmental thinking of the era, were no doubt unacceptable. Trade, economics, financial and commercial considerations were undoubtedly deleted, as were smuggling and many undercover activities. In the Mediterranean, the absence of reference to the Sultan of Morocco, Marshal Lyautey, Bibi Carlton and Juan March is significant.

With regard to concrete matters, two particular lessons may be drawn from the publication of Hall's remaining chapters of his autobiography. One: can any lessons or conclusions concerning today's intelligence needs be drawn by today's intelligence authorities? Two: what lessons might be drawn from the factors influencing America's entry into the war in 1917?

While the first questions can only really be answered by leading intelligence authorities themselves, to help answer the second certain events have only recently emerged.

The evidence in the autobiography represents the British view. Room 40 in London intercepted, decoded and gradually 'leaked' the information from the Zimmermann Telegram to the USA in a way that ensured America would believe it was not a British scam. In this, America's own official representatives in Britain collaborated with the British government.

President Wilson was in difficulty. His moral stance was devoted to isolationism and to avoiding American involvement in the war in Europe. He was being blackmailed and his entire Presidency and reputation hung in the balance. Additionally he was under pressure from certain financial houses and industrial complexes, the former anxious that their loans to the British and French might be impossible for those countries to repay in the event of a German victory; the latter that American industry stood to benefit, and the economy to grow, by their participation in the war.

The American public, with certain exceptions, was totally devoted to isolationism. Even though America was a country populated by a large number of immigrants from Europe, and some remaining pioneer families, there was little desire for people to return to their countries of origin, nor to become actively involved in assisting them.

Bowing to pressure, President Wilson and the American government inaugurated a massive propaganda programme. The controlling body was called the Committee for Public Information and was run by George

Creel, described as 'a muck raking journalist'. It was also known as the Creel Committee.

American accounts of their entry into the war are of two kinds. First there are the official government websites (US Department of State, Office of the Historian: www.history.state.gov) and then the independent websites, such as the Doughboy Center (www.worldwar1.com). They tell rather different stories.

The 'official' reasons as communicated by the Creel Committee were as follows.

1. Unrestricted submarine warfare by Germany (*Lusitania*)
2. Imperial Germany running amok
3. Germany destroying international equilibrium
4. Conflict between the 'democratic nations' and the 'autocratic nations'
5. Isolationism was out of date
6. Germany was a menace to the Monroe Doctrine.

In addition the Creel Committee was made responsible for all the propaganda posters in America, 'Uncle Sam' etc., and for organising speakers and conferences in every state of the Union.

Independently, Doughboy gives the following reasons:

1. Reports of German atrocities, particularly in Belgium
2. Economic benefits to such finance houses as J.P. Morgan, whose $3 billion in loans and bonds to England and France would be lost if Germany or the Central Powers won the war
3. The sinking of the *Lusitania*, even though the German and American authorities knew she was carrying munitions of war. Germany had even advertised this in the US before she set sail
4. Unrestricted submarine warfare, some of it resulting in the sinking of American ships
5. The Zimmermann Telegram.

The Creel Committee policy omitted reference to the Zimmermann Telegram but was, no doubt, reoriented when the media and President Wilson confirmed its authenticity and the splendid role played by the American secret service.

It concentrated more on other issues close to American public interests: the planned invasion of Texas, and other southern states, and the Monroe Doctrine.

American and German historians (Barbara Tuchman and Joachim von zur Gathen, for example) provide evidence from their own national perspectives and, in respect of von zur Gathen, a wealth of up-to-date evidence not previously available. Reconciliation of these various reports and interpretations remains the work of intelligence experts.

NOTES ON THE MAPS AND 'SWEDISH ROUNDABOUT' ROUTE[1]

A word of explanation is called for on the subject of the 'Swedish Roundabout' in Chapter 25. Hall speculated wildly on its possible course of transmission and numerous writers have provided alternative possible routes. These are listed on Maps 5a and 5b. These maps show only the possible dispatch and arrival locations. Valentia (in Ireland), for example, is shown because it was the centre for the densest collection of cable landings (see Map 5a).

---

1   Copyright of the maps in this book is held jointly by Philip Vickers and Katharine Vickers.

The maps are as follows:

Map 1:   Royal Navy coaling stations & bases, First World War
Map 2:   Major Worldwide BNI centres and coastal watch areas
         (excluding Admiralty wireless stations and excluding Europe)
Map 3:   Major European BNI centres and coastal watch areas
Map 4:   BNI pre-First World War secret intelligence missions
Map 5a: The 'Swedish Roundabout' route Europe
Map 5b: The 'Swedish Roundabout' in the Americas.

Route A (Berlin–Sayreville–Washington) is described in *Cryptologia* (31:2–37; 2007) as the 'only [one] in code 0075 over the US Diplomatic lines'. Joachim von zur Gathen also reports on the 'original document never reproduced before' which he reproduces in his account, *The Zimmermann Telegram: The Original Draft*.

We acknowledge the following sources: Andrew, Beesly, Deacon, Freeman, Gannon, James, McKinley, Ramsay, Tuchman, von zur Gathen, West and Wyllie.

The following routes are identified on Maps 5a and 5b:

Route A: Berlin (Nauen/US Embassy)–Sayreville–Washington
Route B: Berlin–Stockholm–Porthcurno–Washington
Route C: Berlin–Stockholm–Porthcurno–Halifax
Route D: Berlin–Stockholm–Copenhagen–Halifax
Route E: Berlin–Stockholm–Buenos Aires–Valparaiso–Mexico
           City–Washington
Route F: Berlin–Buenos Aires–Washington.

Research has indicated that the original actual route is Route A (Gannon, 2010). Prior to this, Route E was the most favoured. Dr von zur Gathen's *Original Draft* document throws more light on the situation.

Von zur Gathen provides evidence under five headings, the most relevant to the 'Roundabout' matter is his point four (proof that the telegram was transmitted from Berlin to Washington only in code 0075 over US diplomatic lines) and especially section 3 of point four: German Options for Encryption and Transmission. His exhaustive research concludes that 'the telegram went to Washington in 0075 over US diplomatic lines, and in no other way'. His 'Swedish Roundabout' section confirms that the largely pro-German Swedes did indeed permit the Germans the use of their diplomatic line. Washington and Buenos Aires were both destinations for Swedish diplomatic traffic. Messages to Buenos Aires reached Washington via Valparaiso to Mexico.

Room 40 read all these messages, thus giving Hall access to the subterfuge he practised on the Americans in order to ensure that they would accept the information. It was feared that America would attribute the source of the telegram to British black propaganda. Had this happened the Zimmermann Telegram would have had no influence on American policy.

For a full understanding of von zur Gathen's analysis the reader is referred to the Taylor & Francis article in the journal *Cryptologia* (31:2–37; 2007).

Zimmermann is said to have communicated with Count Johann von Bernstorff who then communicated the telegram to Heinrich von Eckardt, German Minister in Mexico City. Hall wanted this version as its stamp and serial number would be different from the one intercepted by Room 40. It was here that Tom Hohler became involved.

The numerous alternative routes and the 'subsidiary routes' are listed as Route G: Valentia, Ireland–Wales–London; as Route H: Copenhagen–Newbiggin–London; and as Route I: Madrid–Berlin and are all reported in the literature. This can only serve to underline the complexity of determining the critical route.[2]

The reader is also recommended, for Map 4 (the pre-war secret intelligence missions), to look at the original Walker & Cockerell charts of the Frisian Islands reproduced in 1903 to illustrate Erskine Childers' *The Riddle of the Sands*. For the original charts see nos. 406 and 407 in the British Series and no. 64 of the German Series. The sequence of these missions is as follows: Agent Z, 1901, Emden/Borkum; Trench and Brandon, 1908, Kiel; Hall, 1909, Kiel; Trench & Brandon, 1910, Frisian Islands.

---

2   See *Codebreakers*, James Wyllie and Michael McKinley, Ebury Press/Penguin, Random House, 2015; and *Cryptologia*, Vol. 30, No. 2, Peter Freeman, 2006. For further detail, see Table 16.1, Zimmermann Telegram Time Table, in Gannon's *Inside Room 40*.

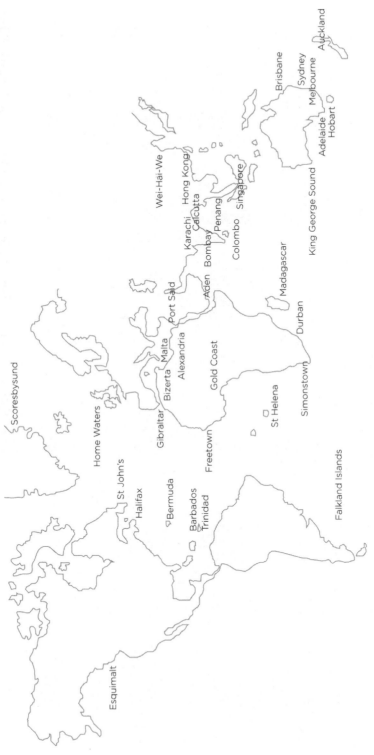

RN Coaling Stations.

Major Room 40 centres worldwide excluding Europe and North Africa.

Siberia

Japan

Persian Gulf

Ascension Island

St Helena

Halifax

New York

Washington

Cuba

Mexico City

Buenos Aires

Falkland Islands

Valparaiso

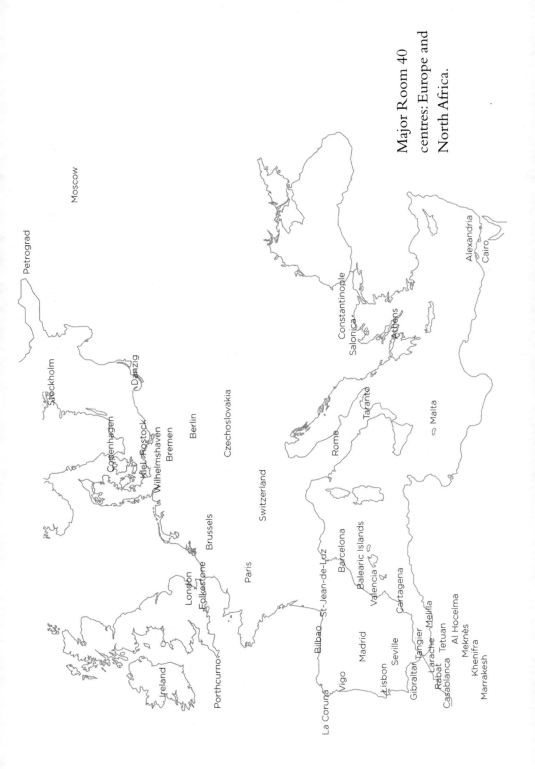

Major Room 40 centres: Europe and North Africa.

Kiel

Hamburg

Heligoland

Bremenshaven

Bremen

Wilhelmshaven

Germany

Frisian Islands

Nordeney

Emden

Juist

Borkum

BNI pre–First World War secret intelligence missions.

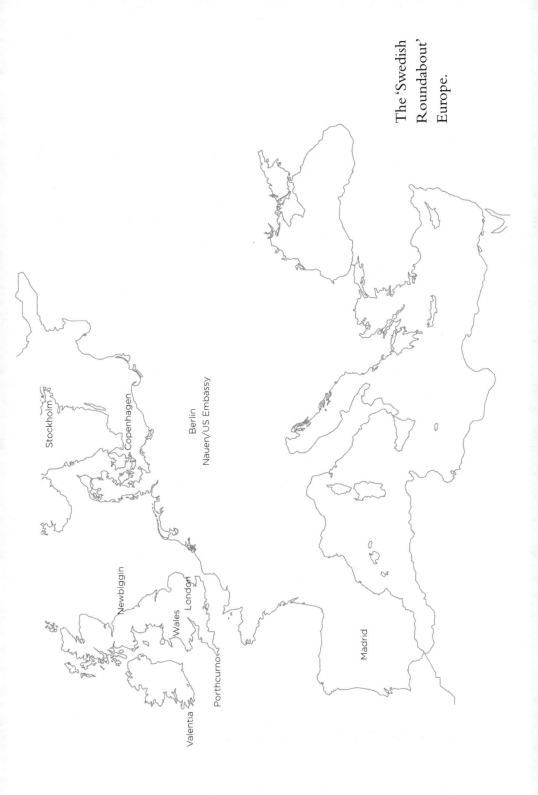

The 'Swedish Roundabout' Europe.

Stockholm

Copenhagen

Berlin
Nauen/US Embassy

Newbiggin

London

Wales

Porthcurno

Valentia

Madrid

The 'Swedish Roundabout': the Americas.

SELECT
BIBLIOGRAPHY

Beach, J., *Haig's Military Intelligence: GHQ and the German Army, 1916–1918* (Cambridge: Cambridge Military History, 2013)

Beesly, P., *Room 40 – British Naval Intelligence 1914–18* (London: Hamish Hamilton, 1982)

Childers, E., *The Riddle of the Sands*, introduction by David Trotter, notes by Anna Smith (Oxford: Oxford World Classics, 1988)

Freeman, P., 'The Zimmermann Telegram Revisited: A Reconciliation of the Primary Sources', *Cryptologia*, Vol. 30, Issue 2, 2006

Gannon, P., *Inside Room 40 – The Codebreakers of World War I* (Hersham: Ian Allan, 2010)

James, W., *The Eyes of the Navy – A Biographical Study of Admiral Sir Reginald Hall* (London: Methuen, 1936)

Judd, A., *The Quest for C – Mansfield Cumming and the Founding of the Secret Service* (London: Harper Collins, 1999)

Kennedy, P., *The Rise of Anglo-German Antagonism* (London: Allen & Unwin, 1980)

Le Queux, *Number 70, Berlin: A Story of Britain's Peril* (London: Hodder & Staughton, 1916)

Massie, R.K., *Dreadnought – Britain, Germany and the Coming of the Great War* (London: Vintage Books, 2007)

Maze, P., *Frenchman in Khaki* (London: Heinemann, 1984)

Ramsay, D., *'Blinker' Hall Spymaster – The Man who Brought America into World War I* (Stroud: The History Press, 2008)

Strachen, H., *The First World War* (London: Simon & Schuster, 2003)

Tuchman, B., *The Zimmermann Telegram* (London: Constable, 1959)

Vickers P., *Finding Thoroton: The Royal Marine Who Ran British Naval Intelligence in the Western Mediterranean in World War One* (Southsea: Royal Marines Historical Society, 2013)

Von zur Gathen, 'The Zimmermann Telegram: The Original Draft', *Cryptologia*, Vol. 31, Issue 2–7, 2007

Watts, A.J., *The Royal Navy – An Illustrated History* (London: Brockhampton Arms & Armour Press, 1999)

West, N., *MI6 – British Secret Intelligence Service Operations 1909–45* (London: Grafton Collins, 1988)

West, N., *MI5 – British Security Service Operations 1909–45* (London: Triad Grafton, 1987)

Wyllie, J. and McKinley, M., *The Codebreakers – The True Story* (London: Ebury Press, 2015)

I would like to acknowledge T S Eliot's *Four Quartets* (New York: Harper Brace, 1945) for my quotation from his poem *The Dry Salvages*.

ACKNOWLEDGEMENTS

My gratitude goes to the many individuals who have contributed immeasurably to this work, and also to the enjoyment of the research and writing. These include notably Mr Timothy Stubbs, the Admiral's grandson, for granting permission for me to write and publish the autobiography. In this I also acknowledge the permission of the Churchill Archives Centre, Cambridge, under Allen Packwood. Nigel West, for his encouragement and extensive expertise. Alfred Blaak, for his IT abilities and historical knowledge which has turned him into a virtual sub-editor. Dr Jim Beach for his generous contribution. Brian Carter RMHS, for his encouraging help in reading the manuscript. I also wish to thank Captain Garth de Courcy-Ireland RN for his perspectives on naval procedures; Simon and Paul Vickers, my two sons, one for his flow of relevant books, the other for his processing contribution; and Christopher Gaisford St Lawrence of Howth for enabling me to visit the various sites of the *Sayonara* on the south coast of Ireland. My cousin Hugo Vickers has well guided me through some complicated issues. Without the tireless assistance of my long-suffering wife Katharine I could not have accomplished this work.

I would also like to thank the contribution made by all the authors listed in the Bibliography, and their publishers. Also those who have courteously presented some of the illustrations. Every effort has been made to make acknowledgement and any omissions should be signalled to the author for subsequent correction. Finally I thank Chrissy McMorris, Commissioning Editor, and Vanessa Le, Project Editor, both at The History Press, for their work in seeing to the completion of the book.

INDEX

222